Group Values
Through
Children's Drawings

Group Values
Through
Children's Drawings

Wayne Dennis
Brooklyn College of the City University of New York

John Wiley & Sons, Inc.
New York   London   Sydney

Preface

In a sense this book began on the Hopi reservation in 1941. It was there and then that I became aware of the differences among cultures which appear in children's drawings and first attempted to understand their significance. My work along these lines was soon interrupted, first by World War II, and then, for a longer period, by my serving as a department chairman, first at the University of Pittsburgh and later at Brooklyn College. Only in recent years have I been able to return to the study of children's drawings as indicators of cultural values.

By tradition and by right, a preface is the place to acknowledge intellectual and charitable debts, obligations that can be discharged only by public confession.

In the course of the work here reported I have incurred many such obligations. Among those to whom I owe thanks, I wish first to mention Marsena Galbreath Dennis, my only wife. To her my gratitude, as well as my ingratitude, is very large. Unfortunately for her, I think aloud, and as a consequence she has been required for years to listen to the painful development of my ideas. In the course of this process, she has made many excellent suggestions, which I have immediately incorporated as my own.

Many other persons have contributed directly or indirectly to this book. Because the total number of contributors is great, only those who have been directly involved in obtaining the drawings, assisting in test administration, or arranging for the gathering of the data can be mentioned by name.

v

Following a geographical sequence, which is often used in this book, I shall acknowledge, in order, the chief persons who rendered assistance in the following countries: the United States, Mexico, Great Britain, Sweden, West Germany, Greece, Turkey, Sudan, Lebanon, Israel, Iran, Cambodia, Formosa (Taiwan), and Japan.

In the United States Dr. Elaine Kinder kindly made available to me drawings by Navaho children which were obtained by the late Morris Steggerda in 1936. This was a particularly important contribution because of its chronological position.

Many American Negro drawings were contributed by Dr. Cecile Finley. The Mississippi Negro drawings were gathered by a graduate student at the University of Mississippi who must remain anonymous but who is aware of my sincere appreciation. Mr. Hertz Frankl introduced me to the Brooklyn Hassidim and was instrumental, as was Benjamin Hulkower, in my obtaining many of the Hassidic drawings.

Most of the New York City drawings to which reference is made in this book were obtained in their own classrooms by teachers enrolled in my graduate classes. In the State of New York only by such illegal means can a drawing be designated as having been made by a child who is a Jew, a Roman Catholic, a Protestant, a Negro, or a white. Therefore, in this case as well as in some others, my helpful accomplices cannot be named.

In Mexico my assistants have been Senora Lourdes de la Torre and Senora Francisca de Mendez.

Professor James Drever of the University of Edinburgh made it possible for me to obtain an unusually extensive collection of drawings from Edinburgh.

In Sweden and in West Germany a former student, now Dr. Kairallah Assar, collected the drawings. He also assisted in the collection of drawings in Syria and Lebanon.

In regard to drawings from schools in Athens, I am grateful to Dr. C. Moustaka for arranging the necessary introductions and permissions and to Mr. Harilaos Dendrinos who served as interpreter and assistant.

My assistant and interpreter in Turkey was Mr. Amer Saray.

The drawings from Sudan, to which references will be made and which contribute much to the illustrations, were gathered by Professor Malik Badri of the American University of Beirut.

Since many drawings have been obtained in Lebanon, my indebtedness in this country is large. I wish to acknowledge the special assistance of Mrs. Yvonne Sayegh, Mrs. Adele Takeiddine, Miss Leila Biksmati, Miss Violet Mirza, Miss Nahid Usayran, and Miss Lucy Abrahamian, and I wish to refer again to the assistance of Dr. Kairallah Assar, who was previously mentioned.

The drawings from Israel were obtained through the good offices of Miss Tova Ben-Dov and Dr. May Bere Merom. Professor Evelyn Raskin of Brooklyn College played an important role in the international diplomacy that was involved.

The primary person who rendered aid in Tehran was Mr. Abbas Hadian of the Iran Department of Education.

The Cambodian drawings were obtained by Professor Helen Brell of Brooklyn College while she was serving as an educational consultant in Cambodia.

Arrangements for obtaining drawings in Taiwan were made by Professor Ivan London of Brooklyn College, who personally directed their collection and who assisted me in their interpretation.

In Japan the administration of the drawing test and the meticulous annotations of the drawings were arranged and supervised by Professor Koji Saito and Dr. Minoru Hiroto, to whom special thanks are due for a valuable collection of

Japanese drawings, only a small part of which has been used.

Over a period of several years Mrs. Mona Carp has been responsible for organizing and labeling my collection of drawings, assisting in the classification of drawings, performing tabulations and computations, and helping in a thousand and one other ways.

Financial aid which has contributed to the preparation of this book has come from the Rockefeller Brothers' Fund, the Social Science Research Council, the U.S. Public Health Service, and the City University of New York.

Finally, I offer my apologies to those whom I have not mentioned, but whom I have not forgotten, including the hundreds of boys and a few girls who contributed the essential drawings.

Wayne Dennis

Brooklyn, New York, September, 1965

Contents

List of Illustrations

Chapter One

Drawings Reflect Values

The purposes of this book are to propose, to demonstrate, and to illustrate a method which we believe can contribute to the understanding of the social values of any group. In any attempt to understand the values of groups, contributions can be made by many kinds of scholars and social scientists: anthropologists, economists, historians, psychologists, sociologists, to mention only a few. In this book we intend to discuss a particular technique, not previously used for this purpose, which we believe can supplement other techniques, namely, the use of children's drawings.

The use of drawings is an indirect method, that is, the child, the teacher, the school officials need not know that values are to be assessed through the classroom collection of drawings. The question arises in an investigation of group values, why not use a direct approach? This is the polling or questionnaire approach. It is useful when it will work, but some groups are unwilling to express their values. In many groups such questions are suspect, and the questioner mistrusted. Even where there are no constraints on questioning, some people are unable to state their views on a topic because of linguistic impoverishment, or because they are unacquainted with some of the alternatives which a question implies. A further handicap to the interrogative approach is that the investigator in formulating his questions may assume a frame of reference on the part of the respondent that is quite unreal.

Is there a method which circumvents these difficulties? We have indicated that we think there is and that it consists in the use of drawings, more specifically of children's drawings, and more specifically still of children's drawings of a man.

At first this idea may seem absurd; how can children's drawings of a man reveal social values? We will attempt to demonstrate that this is possible. Our conviction that drawings are significant in respect to group values is derived not from armchair speculation or from preconceived theories, but from the examination of several thousand drawings, in relation to the known or probable values of the groups from which they came.

When we say that drawings of a man reflect group values, we are referring to the *content* of the drawings. We are not referring to their size, or to the pressure upon the pencil, or to erasures or firmness of line, but to the kinds of men drawn, that is, whether they are soldiers or farmers, bankers or beggars, and so forth. Our proposal is that children generally draw the men whom they admire and who are thought of favorably by their societies. If this is true, children's drawings will reveal the values of their respective groups, in so far as they can be represented visually.

In obtaining drawings, we distribute pencils and blank sheets of paper to a class of school children. We ask them to draw a man, any kind of a man they wish. One can think of the sheet of paper which the child has before him as constituting the purest sort of "projective test." It is like a blank card inserted in the Rorschach Test or the Thematic Apperception Test. The child draws something which is not there. Whereas what he draws originally came from the external world, it has been internalized and is reproduced from the interior, so to speak. We propose that usually he will draw a figure toward which he has positive attitudes. This we will call the value hypothesis.

Many objections can be raised to the proposal that drawings reflect group values. Several objections have been voiced on occasions on which we have presented some of the material contained in this book to graduate seminars and to other audiences. Although we will deal more fully with these criticisms at later points, we wish to discuss some of them in advance.

The interpretation of drawings which seems satisfactory to many people is that when asked to draw a man, a child will draw a man who is immediately before him, either in the flesh or in a picture on the wall. In fact he seldom does so. First of all it should be remarked that sometimes no man or picture of a man is present in the classroom. In many classrooms from which we have obtained data, both the examiner and the teacher were women, and no pictures of men were present. In other instances a male teacher and a male examiner were present, and pictures of men were prominently displayed. No differences appeared between drawings obtained under these two conditions. Under the latter condition very seldom did the pupils attempt to draw the men present, or men whose pictures were present. In drawing a man, children seldom take their eyes from the paper before them and seldom draw a particular individual.

This may be illustrated as follows. In several classrooms we were the examiner. We wore black horn-rimmed glasses. In this situation, only one child drew a picture which resembled us, and very few drew a man who wore glasses. Regardless of whoever is present in the classroom, drawings of children usually depict not those individuals but representatives of classes of men, such as men in modern dress. To repeat, the copy from which a drawing is derived is internal, not immediately present.

The kind of man who is drawn must, of course, have been seen or heard about or read about. But every child has seen many kinds of men, in the flesh or in pictures. Therefore when asked to draw a man, he must make a choice. Because only one kind of man may come to mind, he may be quite unaware that a selection has been made. The child may not know that he is drawing one kind of man in preference to many other kinds which he has seen.

For example, almost all children have seen thin men and fat men, young men and old men, men they consider to be handsome, and men they consider to be ugly. Although each child is acquainted with human differences in respect to body build, age, beauty, and many other dimensions of appearance, when asked to draw a man he can draw only one man. The man drawn cannot be both thin and fat, both young and old, both handsome and ugly. By phrasing these comparisons in terms of dichotomies, we are simplifying the problem, but the principle that choice is unavoidable remains, even if multiple categories are considered. Our hypothesis is that values control to a large extent the kind of man who is portrayed. The man drawn is not merely a familiar man. He is a familiar man toward whom favorable attitudes are held.

All later chapters will be devoted primarily to presenting evidence on this point. We will see that in Middle Eastern countries in which both white collar workers and beggars are known to children, and in which children are encouraged to give coins to beggars, it is the white collar worker, never the beggar, who appears in their drawings. In countries where fat men are common, portly men are seldom drawn today, although probably they would have been in former times and places in which avoirdupois was once a sign of high social status. In other words it is our hypothesis that drawings do not merely mirror the environment. They reflect *values* or *preferences,* not the frequencies of experiences.

Since this proposition is central, let us give one more example of our view in order that the reader will be prepared to consider critically the evidence which we will present. It can be said, with some truth, that drawings reflect culture. But each culture has many aspects. Each culture possesses men who play different social roles, and in most cultures a man plays different roles at different times. A child who draws a man of his own group must make a choice within his culture. If he draws a man who does not belong to his own group, he must make a choice from among various outgroups.

To put the matter another way, we can say that the situation in drawing resembles that in which a dream or a daydream occurs. Within the limits of societal taboos, the sheet of paper before the child provides him with an opportunity for wish fulfillment, that is, on this paper he can symbolically achieve his goals. He can draw a soldier. He can draw a priest. In "real life" he may not be able to become either a soldier or a priest, but he can draw the one he prefers. In other words, we are proposing that in drawing a man children reveal their aspirations and their attitudes. Although we will discuss only drawings which represent persons, we believe that there exists a general principle that children asked to draw a referent which offers a multiplicity of forms usually draw the form which they prefer. That is, if children were asked to draw foods, we believe they would draw favorite foods, not those they dislike. If they were asked to draw plants, they would draw those bearing flowers or fruits, not noxious weeds. We have chosen to have children draw men, rather than foods or plants, because their choices of men have a greater social significance.

Choices of women, too, have social significance, but men occupy more varied social roles, so that in drawing men both boys and girls can display attitudes toward more diverse positions, occupations, religions, recreations, etc., than if they were to draw women. Children's drawings of women are interesting supplements to their drawings of men. We have made a start in this direction which will be reported later. But since we were limited in time and resources we chose to have children draw men because we feel that such drawings yield a greater amount of socially relevant information than drawings of any other referent.

We do not suggest that we can "prove" that the contents

of drawings reflect values. To do so requires independent measures of values, which usually are not available. We are proposing an hypothesis for which there are some positive data and, in our opinion, no negative data. We believe there is no interpretation other than the one that "drawings reflect values" which is able to encompass the findings which we will present. This will be our "proof."

In the preceding pages, emphasis has been placed upon the expression in drawings of positive attitudes. Can drawings indicate negative attitudes as well as positive ones? The answer is yes. If children are familiar with a referent but seldom draw it, in our opinion, they are either not interested in it or are negative toward it, or they are inhibited by a societal taboo against its representation. Our treatment will deal with the absence of certain familiar kinds of men in drawings as well as with the presence of other familiar kinds of men. The figures which are drawn are significant, but that certain figures are not drawn is equally significant. If one knows both faces of a coin and sees which face is upward, he knows what is hidden.

Negative attitudes toward certain kinds of men can be expressed not only by the absence of such men in drawings, but also by negative distortion, that is, a man may be drawn in a manner which shows that he is being ridiculed. This is a technique which is used by cartoonists and caricaturists. We shall see that children seldom use this technique. This may be because they lack the required degree of skill, or because they are more interested in expressing positive goal figures than in depicting negative ones. Figures which indicate a negative attitude are seldom drawn by children under fourteen years. Since most of our subjects are under age fourteen, we will have little occasion to deal with drawings which indicate negative attitudes toward the referent, but one chapter will be devoted to this topic.

We have indicated that we believe that the drawings of

children show not only the values of children but also the values of their societies. This is because most of the values which children hold are communicated to them. Most communication is downward from the older to the younger. Even when there are age differences in values, these age norms also are communicated from above. If this is a correct interpretation, the study of children's drawings provides information not only about children but also about the older children and the adults with whom they are affiliated.

The reader will have noted that in speaking of attitudes and values we have referred to the attitudes and values of groups, not to the attitudes and values of individuals. This will be our emphasis throughout this book. In this investigation, we are not attempting to study the values of individuals. In our opinion the study of the group leads to much more valid results than does the study of the individual. For example, from actuarial experience one can predict fairly accurately the suicide rate of a group during the current year, but it is difficult to determine which particular individuals will commit suicide.

The knowledgeable reader knows that other persons have made use of children's drawings of a man for other purposes than the one here proposed. The two persons most prominently involved in such studies have been Florence Goodenough (1926), who used children's drawings of a man to obtain a measure of individual "intelligence," and Karen Machover (1948), who has used drawings of a person to assist in the assessment of individual personality. We will not attempt to evaluate either of these methods, positively or negatively. They are irrelevant to the value hypothesis. We are concerned here with a *third* use of drawings which is only loosely related to those of Goodenough and Machover. We wish our interpretation to be considered on its own merits, whatever decision may be reached concerning the merits of drawings as measures of intelligence or personality.

Critics may point out that drawings do not reveal all kinds of social values. Let us be the first to acknowledge the legitimacy of this criticism. Drawings can represent only the visible aspects of the person. They cannot reveal what cannot be seen. They cannot be heard, smelled, or tasted. They do not move, are not linguistic, and reflect only values which can be represented graphically. A further weakness of this technique is that its utility is limited by the skill of the artist. Perhaps a boy may admire a sprinter running the 100-yard dash, but boys of eleven, twelve, or thirteen years often are not able to draw a man doing a sprint.

Because skill is related to culture, in societies in which representational art is only slightly developed human figure drawings with significant content cannot be expected. For example, we have found (Dennis, 1958) that in drawings of a man made by Bedouin boys there is little content which reveals social attitudes, because the drawings are crude and have few details. But some indicators of social values can be drawn even by persons who have little proficiency in drawing. For example, kindergarten children in the United States often draw men with smiles. Few kindergarten children in other countries do so. This difference in content can be demonstrated not to be a difference in artistic skill.

No tool can perform all functions, and neither can any test. We do not propose that drawings reveal all group values. The problem is to learn what they do reveal; this we shall attempt to determine.

Chapter Two

How and Where
Drawings Were Obtained

Procedure in Testing

Except when otherwise stated, the drawings to which reference will be made were obtained from children attending school and were made in their usual classrooms. All drawings were made under the supervision of a person other than the teacher. Experience has shown us that many teachers, unless restrained, cannot control the urge to tell children what and how to draw, perhaps by placing a model on the blackboard or by suggesting the kind of person to be drawn. Such directions, of course, defeat the purpose of our study. For this reason an examiner, who was either the present writer, another psychologist, or a trained assistant was always present and in charge of the class when the children were making drawings. At times the teacher, the principal, or another school administrator also was present, but in every case a supervising examiner who understood the local language monitored the situation.

In order to minimize advance briefing or coaching, whenever it was possible drawings were collected without prior knowledge, on the part of school officials, that drawings were to be obtained. This was done by the examiner appearing at the school without an appointment. We, or our assistant, explained that we were making an international collection of children's drawings and that we would like to include in our collection drawings from the children of this school. We asked permission to obtain drawings on that day, if it were possible. Usually permission was given.

Within the classroom, sheets of white 8½ in. x 11 in. paper were distributed, and No. 2 pencils with erasers were provided to students who needed them. Students were asked not to use ink or crayons.

The students were told: "On these sheets of paper, I want each of you to draw a picture of a man. You may draw any kind of man you wish, but draw a whole man, not just the head and shoulders. You may have as much time as you need. Do you have any questions?"

Most questions asked by the students could be answered by repeating part of the instructions. If a child indicated that he could not draw a man, he was assured that every child can draw a man. The participation was usually 100 per cent.

Although there was no fixed time limit for completing the drawings, slow children were urged to hurry so as not to keep the class waiting to resume its usual schedule. Papers were collected as the individual children indicated they had completed their drawings.

While the drawings were being made, the assistant and the author, if he was present, moved about the classroom to try to insure that aids such as rulers (to make straight lines) and compasses, ink bottles and coins (to make round heads) were not being used, but nevertheless some children succeeded in evading our supervision, particularly in classrooms of forty to fifty children.

Before he turned in his drawing each child was asked to place his name and age at the top of his paper. The name served to indicate the sex of the student and to identify the child in case we wished later to ask him questions concerning the man he had drawn.

In the main we chose for testing those classes in which the most common ages were eleven, twelve, and thirteen years. These age levels were chosen for several reasons. One reason was that children of these ages can draw better than can younger children, and therefore more of the kinds of men drawn by older children are identifiable. Secondly, in many communities the school drop-out rate becomes high beyond age thirteen. For this reason, pupils older than thirteen years often represent a selected group of students. In contrast to older pupils, the eleven-, twelve-, thirteen-year-old children who are in school often comprise all of the children of these ages in their communities.

In addition to obtaining drawings from children of these age levels, in some schools we obtained drawings from younger and older children. In some instances we obtained drawings not only from lower grades but also from high school students, and even from college students. But in the chapters which follow, unless exceptions are noted, our data will refer to drawings obtained in classes consisting primarily of eleven-, twelve-, and thirteen-year-olds.

When it was possible, drawings by children of these ages in a school system or in a community were combined so as to form a total of 100. This was done to simplify the presentation of results, that is, to avoid the necessity of making repetitious statements concerning the size of each group.

In large schools in which more than one hundred children were tested, 100 drawings were selected by chance and retained. In small communities it was sometimes necessary to include some ten-year-olds and fourteen-year-olds in order to obtain a total of 100. There are a few groups, to be indicated later, in which a total of 100 boys was not obtained. In every group listed as one of the "main" groups the median age of the boys was between 12.0 and 13.0 years.

Our "main groups" of drawings were obtained in the following countries: the United States, Mexico, Great Britain, Sweden, West Germany, Greece, Turkey, Lebanon, Israel, Iran, Cambodia, Japan, and Taiwan. In several of these countries drawings were obtained from several different ethnic groups, and from both public and private schools, or from both poor and well-to-do neighborhoods. The choice of countries in which drawings were to be collected depended upon two factors: the availability of a qualified person who could gather the drawings or assist us in doing so, and the possibility that the drawings would make our sample more heterogeneous.

The drawings on which this report is based are on file in our office. Any responsible investigator who, for scientific purposes, wishes to verify any of our tabulations, or wishes to use our data for further research, is invited to do so. It is hoped that a more permanent archive for drawings can be established at some later date.

The Main Groups

Most of the drawings to which we refer come from the 27 groups listed below, but, as we have indicated, some references are made to drawings from other groups.

At the end of the description of each group figures in parentheses indicate the number of drawings and the year or years in which they were obtained.

1. *Brooklyn white Christians.* Boys who are Christian but not Negro, Puerto Rican, or Oriental. Both Protestants and Catholics were included. Most of the Protestants were in public schools, most of the Catholics were in parochial schools. All came from lower-middle-class and lower-class neighborhoods. National origins include Great Britain, Ireland, Italy, Norway, and Sweden (100; 1962).

2. *Brooklyn Negroes.* These Negroes were attending integrated public schools in low socioeconomic areas (65; 1962).

3. *Mississippi Negroes.* Negro boys attending segregated schools in Oxford, Mississippi, and in nearby rural areas (100; 1962).

4. *Brooklyn public school Jewish boys.* These children were identified by their teachers as being Jewish. They are

assumed to be nonorthodox because they were attending public schools (100; 1956).

5. *Brooklyn Yeshiva boys.* Boys attending Jewish parochial schools (Yeshivas) (100; 1962).

6. *Brooklyn Hassidim.* These are boys from an ultra-conservative Jewish group located in the Williamsburg area of Brooklyn (see Poll, 1962). They are children of post-World War II immigrants, chiefly from Hungary. A fuller description will be presented in connection with the discussions of their drawings (100; 1962).

7. *Navaho Indians.* Boys attending government Indian schools on the Navaho reservation (100; 1936).

8. *Mexico City.* Children of varying degrees of European and Indian ancestry in Mexico City. Both public and private schools are represented (100; 1962).

9. *San Cristobal.* Children of varying degrees of European and Indian ancestry living in the town of San Cristobal in the state of Chiapas, Mexico. They were attending public schools in the "better" areas (100; 1964).

10. *Chiapas Indians.* Indian boys from the Chamula and Zinecanteco groups attending rural schools near San Cristobal, Mexico (100; 1964).

11. *Edinburgh.* Boys from a lower-class and lower-middle-class government school in Edinburgh (100; 1963. Four hundred drawings were obtained, but most of our statistics will refer only to a subsample of 100).

12. *Gothenburg.* Boys from a government school in Gothenburg, Sweden (40; 1963).

13. *Heidelburg.* Boys from a middle-class school in Heidelburg, Germany (100; 1963).

14. *Athens.* Boys from one government and one private school in Athens, Greece (70; 1963).

15. *Beirut.* Arab boys attending a private school associated with the American University of Beirut, Lebanon (100; 1955 and 1963).

16. *Lebanese villages I.* Boys from three relatively progressive villages in Lebanon (100; 1958 and 1964).

17. *Lebanese villages II.* Boys from three poor and relatively isolated villages (100; 1958).

18. *Armenian Lebanese.* Armenian boys attending Armenian schools in Beirut and in the village of Ainjar (75; 1964).

19. *Ankara.* Boys, some in private and some in government schools, in Ankara, Turkey (100; 1958).

20. *Nonorthodox Israelis.* Boys attending nonreligious government schools in Haifa and Tel Aviv. They are chiefly of European ancestry (100; 1958).

21. *Orthodox Israelis.* Boys attending Orthodox schools in two Israeli villages and in Tel Aviv. They are chiefly of Middle Eastern ancestry (100; 1958).

22. *Tehran.* Boys attending government schools in one poor and one middle-class neighborhood in Tehran (100; 1959).

23. *Cambodia.* Boys in a government school in a village not far from Phnom Penh (100; 1958).

24. *Kyoto.* Boys in government schools in Kyoto, Japan (100; 1959).

25. *A Japanese village.* Boys attending government schools in a relatively isolated Japanese mountain village (100; 1959).

26. *Taipei I.* Boys of the upper and upper-middle classes in government schools in Taipei, Taiwan (Republic of China) (100; 1964).

27. *Taipei II.* Boys of lower-middle and lower-class families attending government schools in Taipei (100; 1964).

In the above listing there are twenty-three groups of one hundred and four groups of less than one hundred. They produced a total of 2550 drawings.

The arrangement of groups as listed above is geographical. It starts with the United States and Mexico and moves eastward through Great Britain, Europe, and the Near East to Eastern Asia. The reader is reminded that all of these groups consist of boys, and all were asked to draw a man. In Chapter 14 we will also consider some drawings by girls who were asked to draw a woman.

Chapter Three

Some Widespread Preferences

Although this book is concerned primarily with differences among groups in respect to their values, the uniformities among groups as well as their diversities are pertinent to the thesis that drawings reflect values since some values may be quasi-universal.

At the present time, to talk of universal human traits is not popular among behavioral scientists, because in the past so many human characteristics once alleged to be universal have been shown to belong chiefly to a specific area. However, among the groups from which we have obtained drawings it appears that certain aspects of children's preferences are very widespread. They may be universal, but further studies may show that they are not.

We present in Table 1 data on ten aspects of appearance that we have found can be classified reliably (inter-rater agreement of 98 per cent or greater) as present or absent. The list of such traits could be extended, but our aim is to expound and illustrate a principle, not to conduct all of the possible analyses to which the principle may lead.

Each line of Table 1 indicates both for each group and for the total twenty-seven groups the relative frequencies of two alternative ways of drawing a certain aspect of a man. In respect to each of these aspects of the drawings, we have chosen to present in Table 1 the incidence of the less frequently drawn trait in terms of the per cent of the drawings in which it is present. The frequency of the more popular alter-

Table 1 Per Cents of Drawings Containing Ten Unpopular Characteristics

	Brooklyn White Christians	Brooklyn Negroes	Mississippi Negroes	Brooklyn Public School Jews	Brooklyn Yeshivas	Brooklyn Hassidim	Navahos	Mexico City	San Cristobal	Chiapas Indians	Edinburgh	Gothenburg	Heidelberg	Athens	Beirut	Lebanese villages I	Lebanese villages II	Ankara	Lebanese Armenians	Israeli nonorthodox	Israeli Orthodox	Tehran	Cambodia	Kyoto	Japanese village	Taipei I	Taipei II	Totals
1. Old	0	2	0	0	1	0	1	0	0	5	0	0	0	0	0	0	0	0	0	0	0	0	0	3	0	5	3	18
2. Spectacles	2	3	0	2	4	5	1	0	1	1	1	1	7	2	1	2	0	1	0	2	1	0	1	27	10	1	3	77
3. Cross-eyed	0	0	0	2	1	0	0	0	0	1	0	0	0	1	2	0	0	0	0	0	0	1	0	1	0	1	0	9
4. Facial scars	0	0	0	0	0	1	0	0	0	0	0	0	0	0	0	0	0	0	0	0	0	0	0	0	0	0	0	0
5. Mouth corners down	0	0	0	1	0	0	0	0	0	0	0	0	1	0	0	1	1	0	0	0	0	0	0	0	0	1	0	5
6. Tattooed	0	0	0	0	0	0	0	0	0	0	0	0	1	0	0	0	0	0	0	0	0	0	0	0	0	0	0	1
7. Crippled	0	0	0	0	0	0	0	0	0	0	0	1	1	0	0	1	0	0	0	0	0	0	0	0	0	0	0	0
8. Fat	0	0	0	0	1	0	0	0	1	1	1	0	0	0	0	0	0	0	0	0	0	0	0	0	0	0	0	3
9. Patched clothing	2	0	0	0	0	0	0	0	0	1	0	0	0	0	0	0	0	1	0	0	0	0	0	0	7	1	3	15
10. Eye patch	0	0	1	0	0	0	0	0	0	0	1	0	1	0	0	0	0	0	0	0	0	0	0	0	0	0	0	2

native is 100 per cent minus the per cent reported in Table 1.

By item 1, old men, we refer to drawings which represent men with one or more aspects of appearance which are often possessed by old men but seldom possessed by young men. Specifically, these are a bald head, a wrinkled face, or a stooped posture.

Most boys, eleven, twelve, and thirteen years of age, draw men who are young or, at most, middle-aged. Line 1 of Table 1 shows that only eighteen boys in 2550 drew men who were old. This is, of course, less than 1 per cent of the total. We classified men as old on the basis of baldness only in drawings in which men are portrayed as having hair around the edge of the scalp, but not on the top of the scalp. That is, if in a drawing a man had no hair at all, we did not classify him as being old, because such a drawing may merely indicate a low degree of drawing skill, unless other aspects of the drawing show this not to be the case. Figure 1 shows a Brooklyn man who is undoubtedly bald, and Figure 2, a Japanese man who is bald but is classified as old for other reasons as well.

The infrequency of drawings of old men, in our opinion, is not the expression of a specific aversion to old age. The data which follow will show that it is an instance of a general aversion to men who have defects, whether the defects are due to age, deformity, injury, or sickness.

In Table 1, line 2 indicates for each group, and for the total of the drawings, how many men with spectacles are drawn. As the table shows, in many groups the number of men drawn with spectacles is zero. In general, except for the Kyoto group, spectacles in drawings are infrequent. Among the total number, it is 3 per cent. However, among Kyoto children 27 per cent drew men with eyeglasses. Figure 3 represents a man wearing spectacles, drawn by a Kyoto boy. Although bespectacled men in Kyoto drawings are in the minority, the relatively high frequency of spectacles in Kyoto drawings requires attention.

Let us first note that spectacles ordinarily signify the presence of a visual defect. However, since eyeglasses are most frequently worn by literate persons and by those who can afford them, they may become associated with persons of the higher social groups. Why Kyoto children so often put eyeglasses on their men may be explained by a quotation from Keizo (1958).

In the Meiji period [which began in 1867] there was a large new demand for eyeglasses on the part of officials, students, and teachers who spent much of their time poring over books, and the demand was further increased by others who wished to appear as though they spent much of their time poring over books. The fad for glasses among those whose eyes were perfectly good was apparently quite widespread for a time.

The "Record of Enlightenment and Prosperity in Tokyo" speaks sarcastically of people wearing spectacles to keep dust out of their eyes, and a policeman in Gifu is recorded to have asked the head of the prefectural hospital whether the practice among intellectuals of growing long hair was not an affectation "like the practice among healthy people of wearing glasses."

Spectacles must have grown fairly common during the period, but people over seventy remember that a person wearing glasses was often described as looking like an official. Actually, it is likely that a relatively high proportion of the people who needed glasses were indeed officials, and it is therefore not surprising that in this age of reverence for anything governmental many persons adopted glasses for show.

In a large city like Kyoto, where one has a great degree of anonymity, one can wear glasses with only a slight chance of being challenged concerning his education or occupation. In a village in which almost all men are known by all to be farmers, or woodcutters, the drawing of a man with spectacles may seem inappropriate and may be ridiculed. This is perhaps the reason why, although spectacles are present in 27 per cent of the Kyoto drawings, only 10 per cent of the Japanese village boys drew men with spectacles. In addition, the tradition that spectacles represent high social status may be more commonly known and accepted by children in a larger urban center than it is in a small, isolated village in which there are few, if any, persons of high status. In a fishing village, not represented in Table 1, spectacles were even less frequently depicted than in the village represented in Table 1.

As we noted in Chapter 1, children do not draw spectacles because they see a person in spectacles when drawings are being made. To repeat a former statement, we were in the classroom, standing before the class or moving from desk to desk, when eleven of the main groups were being tested. We wore black horn-rimmed glasses, yet in these eleven groups, which do not include the Japanese groups, fewer than one child in one hundred drew a man with spectacles. This probably shows that spectacles are unpopular in these groups, not necessarily that we were unpopular.

Line 3 of Table 1 shows the frequency of cross-eyed men in the drawings of each group. In all groups combined only nine boys—one third of 1 per cent—drew a cross-eyed man. Figure 4 presents one of these figures, drawn by a Kyoto boy.

The possibility exists that in some cases the drawing of a cross-eyed man was not intentional but was the result of poor drawing skill. Another possibility is that some of these drawings were intended to ridicule. In other words, no drawing of a cross-eyed man need be assumed to express admiration.

Item 4, Facial scars, has a zero frequency. It is significant that in none of the groups represented in Table 1 do facial scars have a favorable significance. But facial scars in the Sudan (not a "main group" and therefore not in Table 1) formerly showed tribal affiliation and formerly also showed status since slaves were not permitted to adorn themselves with self-inflicted facial scars. Through the courtesy of Professor Malik Badri of the American University of Beirut, himself a Sudanese, we are able to reproduce a drawing of a man with scars (Figure 5) made by a Sudanese child. Although facial scars are drawn by some Sudanese children, the proportion of them who draw men with facial scars is small. This may be because today men with facial scars are usually older men and because at present in most communities the practice of scarification is not approved.

As shown in line 5, in few groups are faces shown with the corners of the mouth pulled down, (see Figure 6 for a Lebanese village II example and Figure 7 for a Taipei I illustration). There are five such drawings in 2550. It appears that mouth corners down is not a generally approved behavior.

We proceed now to line 6 of Table 1, Tattooed. In New York, and we presume that this is generally true in modern societies, tattooed figures are worn chiefly by men of the lower social classes. Only one boy, a Heidelburg pupil, drew a man with a tattooed figure (Figure 8). We shall have occasion to note that other indicators of low social status are seldom drawn.

It can be assumed that no one wishes to have an amputated arm or leg or to be crippled in any other way. In 2550 drawings no crippled man was drawn (see line 7 of Table 1). Obviously, we can reproduce no figure of a crippled man.

In many societies men who are fat are ridiculed. It is not surprising, therefore, that only three boys drew fat men (see line 8 of Table 1). These drawings may have been drawn to express ridicule (for an example, see Figure 9).

Just as few men wish to be fat, so few men wish to be poor. One sign of poverty is to wear clothing that is patched. Only fifteen boys drew men with patches (see line 9). Seven of these boys were Japanese (see Figure 10). The Japanese boys in general give great attention to detail in their drawings. It may be that patches were drawn to show artistic virtuosity rather than to indicate an admiration of poverty.

It should be noted that several of our groups of boys were poor. Certainly, patches on clothing are not unknown to Mississippi Negro boys or to boys in poor Lebanese villages. Yet not one of these boys drew a man with patched clothing.

Line 10 in Table 1 shows the incidence of drawings of men wearing an eye patch. Two men were drawn with a patch over one eye; one example can be seen in Figure 11. As the reader can see, this figure is somewhat glamorous and does not obviate the possibility that it may be admired. No totally blind men were drawn.

In preceding paragraphs, we noted that there were no crippled men and no men with facial scars in our main groups. Except for those, we have not referred to other kinds of men who are *never* drawn. "Never" refers, of course, only to the universe of drawings with which we are familiar, but we should mention that within the realm of our experience we have not seen drawings of the following: men with one arm, one leg, or with no arms or no legs, men with partially amputated limbs or fingers, men with one ear, men with missing teeth, men with a physiognomy which indicates a cleft palate, men who have been hanged, men in coffins, or other corpses. Without doubt, the kinds of men who have *not* been drawn could be extended. We wish only to make the point that some kinds of men, in our experience, are *never* drawn. They represent conditions which very generally meet with avoidance or abhorrence. What are the alternative explanations for the absence of drawings of these men? It would seem to require no more skill to draw a man with one arm or one leg than to draw a man with two arms or two legs, but the former is not done, except in obviously incomplete drawings by young children.

In our opinion the data represented in Table 1 and the findings just discussed support strongly our interpretation that boys draw men who are admired figures, seldom men who for various reasons are not admired.

That the items shown in Table 1 are seldom drawn because they are difficult for boys of ages eleven, twelve, and thirteen years to draw could be answered by asking them to draw an old man, a crippled man, a man with an eye patch and so forth. We have not done this, because the uniformities shown in Table 1 became apparent to us only after the collection of our data was completed.

There are certain internal kinds of evidence which tend to show that lack of skill is not the cause of the infrequencies of the items which are seldom drawn. For example, it seems to require no more skill to draw a cross-eyed man than it does to draw a man who is not cross-eyed. The difference lies only in the placement of the pupils. As we have indicated earlier, the presence of a few cross-eyed men in our drawings may be the result of *lack* of skill.

In considering item 5, Mouth corners down, which has a total frequency of 5, let us anticipate a later chapter by noting that many children drew the corners of the mouth turned *up*. We do not believe that it requires more skill to draw the mouth curved downward than to draw it turned upward. Consider one more instance: many of the Japanese children who did *not* draw men with spectacles or patches nevertheless drew men with pockets, fountain pens, wrist watches, and brief cases. The Japanese drawings are particularly skillful; without doubt the children who drew men with pockets, pens, and watches could have drawn men with spectacles or patches.

An alternative to the value hypothesis in accounting for the infrequency of many kinds of men in drawings is the familiarity hypothesis. This interpretation holds that children draw that which is most familiar to them. In respect to Table 1, it is true that bald-headed men are less common in a child's experience than men with hair, men with spectacles are less frequently seen than men without them, etc. If our evidence for the value interpretation depended entirely upon Table 1, we would not be able to reject the familiarity hypothesis, because the kinds of men represented in Table 1 are in fact less frequently seen in most societies than are their respective alternatives. But we feel that other data to be presented later argue conclusively against the familiarity hypothesis because, as we shall see, some groups draw the less familiar of two alternative kinds of men. On this point we respectfully request the reader to withhold judgment until further evidence is presented.

We have examined ten instances in which a child drawing a man must represent him as having or not having a certain aspect of appearance, such as having or not having spectacles, or crossed-eyes, or tatoo marks. In each case, the alternative which is presumed to represent a goal figure to most boys is more frequently drawn. When the contrasting figure is drawn, there are reasons to suppose that the unpopular alternative, such as an eye patch, may be favored by some boys, and that in other instances, such as the drawing of a man with crossed-eyes, the drawing of the unusual alternative may be due to poor artistic proficiency. In other words, the amount of evidence supporting the value hypothesis is large insofar as the widespread preferences shown in Table 1 are concerned, but it also supports the familiarity hypothesis.

*Figure 1   A bald-headed man drawn by a Brooklyn
Jewish boy in a public school.*

Figure 2   An old Japanese man.

Figure 3   A Japanese man with spectacles.

Figure 4   A cross-eyed Japanese man.

28

Figure 5   A Sudanese with facial scars.

Figure 6   A "corners down" Lebanese drawing.

30

Figure 7   A "corners down" Taipei drawing.

31

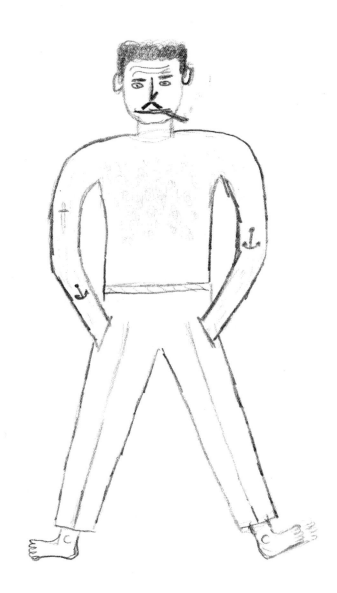

Figure 8   The only man with tattoo marks (Heidelberg).

Figure 9   A fat man drawn by a Heidelberg boy.

33

Figure 10   A Japanese man in patched clothing.

34

Figure 11   A man with an eye patch drawn by a Heidelberg boy.

35

Chapter Four

Modern Dress and Traditional Dress

Men in Modern Dress

In each of our main groups the man most often depicted, if he wears a distinguishable costume, is in modern dress. The terms, dress and costume, as used in this chapter refer to the readily changeable aspects of a man's appearance which include the treatment of cranial and facial hair as well as clothing.

We define modern dress as consisting of the clothing which most men in modern societies wear when shopping, visiting friends, attending social occasions, religious services, or public meetings. It consists usually of having the hair trimmed at the edges of the scalp and of wearing a shirt or sport shirt, a belt, trousers, and shoes. Hat, tie, and coat may be worn but are not necessary in order for a man to be classified as being in modern dress. We also classify as modern dress any other modern costume, such as a football, or baseball or basketball uniform, a police uniform, etc., that is, any costume which can clearly be recognized as characteristic of modern societies rather than folk groups or former societies.

In the accompanying illustrations several figures are presented which show men in modern dress. Figure 12 represents a man in modern dress drawn by a Brooklyn white Christian; Figure 13 was drawn by a boy in Mexico City; Figure 14, by an Edinburgh boy; Figure 15, by a Gothenberg boy; Figure 16, by an Israeli boy; Figure 17, by an Athenian boy; Figure 18, by an Ankara boy; Figure 19, by a Beirut boy; and Figure

20, by a Tehran boy. These drawings should sufficiently illustrate what is meant by "modern dress." The majority of our drawings are like those just shown.

What is the alternative to modern dress? It is a traditional costume which is still worn in the child's own group or which preceded by only a few decades the adoption of modern dress. Children sometimes draw men belonging to an historical period much earlier than today, such as Roman soldiers, or they may draw men in the traditional costume of some group not their own. These are not classified as "traditional." We use the term "traditional" here only for own-group traditional costumes which are currently worn or were recently worn.

Not classified as either modern or traditional are generalized human figures without a costume, figures which cannot be identified in respect to costume, or figures wearing costumes neither modern or traditional. This chapter will deal only with the relative frequencies of men in modern and traditional costumes occurring among those drawings which can definitely be classified as representing men in one or the other of these modes of dress.

The reader is well aware that within the past century many groups have discarded traditional dress in favor of modern dress. The wearing of modern dress is part of an encompassing change which may be called "modernization." In our view the boy who draws a modern costume prefers not only modern dress but in all likelihood other, less visible, aspects of modern life. It is our premise that when the children of an ethnic group, most of whose members still preponderantly wear the traditional costume, draw men in modern costume, further cultural change will occur. In other words, the frequency of modern men in boys' drawings should provide an index of modernization as a goal.

The application of this hypothesis is exemplified in a recent paper by Badri and Dennis (1964) dealing with Sudan.

Sudan has two relatively modern cities, Omdurman and Khartoum. There are some villages near these urban centers, and many far removed from them. In every part of Sudan men in modern dress such as teachers or government workers, are familiar to children, but even in modern Sudanese cities the majority of men wear the traditional *galabia,* a long, un-belted cotton gown like a nightgown, extending from the shoulders to the ankles (see Figure 21). In modern urban Sudanese schools the proportion of classifiable drawings which portray men in modern dress is 85 per cent; in remote villages it is 5 per cent. The scores of other groups are appropriately arranged between these values.

In few countries from which we have examined extensive collections of drawings is the regional contrast between modern dress and traditional dress as sharp as in Sudan. In fact, in no other group whose drawings we have examined does traditional dress predominate in drawings even among village children. This finding, however, may be due to the limited range of our collection. There is no reason to suppose that the Sudanese findings could not be duplicated in other groups, particularly other African groups.

Table 2 indicates the per cent of drawings of men in traditional dress among those of our main groups which have a traditional dress. As we have indicated, the per cents in Table 2 refer to the per cent of traditional costumes among those which are classified as traditional or modern.

In respect to incidence of traditional dress in drawings in our main groups, the highest in the table are the Brooklyn Hassidim. They are chiefly post-World War II immigrants from Hungary who are dedicated to preserving what they consider to be the pious way of Jewish life. This way of life, among other things, prescribes for males the wearing of curls before the ears, the wearing of a black, broad-brimmed hat and, as early as possible, the growing of a full beard. These features are rather easily portrayed. Figure 22 provides an example. This drawing was made by a Brooklyn Hassidic boy only ten years old.

It should be noted that despite the attempt on the part of the community to keep the boys firmly rooted in tradition only 35 per cent of the classifiable drawings of Hassidic boys of ages eleven to thirteen years represent men of traditional Hassidic appearance; that is, 65 per cent are modern. If our interpretation is correct, many Hassidic boys will "defect" in the near future.

In the district in which the Hassidim live, they are outnumbered by Negroes and Puerto Ricans who are distinguishable from the Hassidim by skin color, hair texture, by the wearing of moustaches and chin beards in contrast to the full beards of the Hassidim, and by their clothing; nevertheless, no Hassidic boy drew a Puerto Rican or a Negro. It is relevant to note that recently there has been considerable friction between the Hassidim and the Negro and Puerto Rican groups.

In second place on Table 2 are the Zinecanteco and Chamula Indians in the state of Chiapas in Mexico. In many

Table 2   Per Cents of Men Drawn in Traditional Dress

35	Brooklyn Hassidim	21	Israeli Orthodox
34		20	
33		19	
32		18	
31		17	Taipei I
30	Zinecanteco and Chamula Indians	*	
29		*	
28		*	
27		11	Taipei II
26		10	
25	Navaho Indians	9	Japanese village
24		8	
23		7	
22		6	Kyoto

respects these Indians live much as did their pre-Columbian ancestors. Furthermore their distinctive costumes are easy to draw. A Chamula in traditional dress is shown in Figure 23; the Zinecanteco costume is similar but can be distinguished from the Chamula costume. At this point a discussion of the social situation in the state of Chiapas is required.

These two Indian groups just mentioned live near San Cristobal, which is non-Indian. This town was established by the Spanish in 1528. Many of the families in San Cristobal today have Spanish ancestors who came to San Cristobal more than four centuries ago; they still speak Spanish. They follow urban occupations. Very few are engaged in agriculture. They wear modern dress and call themselves Ladinos.

The fundamental social distinction in the state of Chiapas is the distinction between Ladinos and Indians. This is neither a racial nor a caste distinction. It is based on a combination of residence (urban versus rural), language (Spanish versus an Indian tongue), and dress (modern versus an Indian costume).

Those classified socially as Indians are almost solely Indian in blood. The Ladinos, on the other hand, vary from "pure" Caucasians to fullblood Indians, with a large part of the population consisting of a mixture of these two races. A person who is racially Indian can become a Ladino by meeting the required criteria in respect to language, residence, and occupation. However, he usually enters the Ladino group at the bottom of the social scale, for example, as a servant or manual laborer.

Although many Ladinos are poor, whatever their economic status Ladinos consider themselves superior to the Indians. In fact, Ladinos hold all of the governmental, commercial, religious, and educational positions in San Cristobal —all of the positions requiring education.

Their dominance over the Indians is evident in many ways. In stores in San Cristobal (all operated by Ladinos) a

Ladino is given preference in service over an Indian even if the Indian entered before him. Ladinos have Indian servants and workers, but Ladinos do not work for Indians. When an Indian meets a Ladino on a narrow sidewalk, he often steps down to let the Ladino pass. There is no segregation in buses or in the one cinema in the town or in restaurants, but few Indians use these facilities. The distinction between Ladinos and Indians has been in existence for more than four hundred years, and is very much in effect today.

For our hypothesis it is important to emphasize that Indians and Ladinos are very much aware of distinctions in appearance, since each sees the other daily. Because no other towns are near, the Zinecantecos and Chamulas must sell their products in San Cristobal and must buy certain necessities there. Early each morning the Indians bring to San Cristobal vegetables, wood, charcoal, and other products, usually carried on their backs. Many Ladinos in San Cristobal could not exist without this trade. In San Cristobal each day is a market day. In daytime hours Indians outnumber Ladinos on the streets. Because of this all Ladino children are thoroughly familiar with Indian costumes, since they must necessarily pass Indians when going to and returning from school, doing chores, going to see friends, and when going to church.

Whom do Ladino children draw when asked to draw a man? One of our main groups is a San Cristobal Ladino group. In addition we have obtained drawings from younger Ladino children in San Cristobal and from high school pupils. The total number of Ladino drawings collected in San Cristobal exceeds 400. Not one drawing represents an Indian.

No Ladino boy wishes to hold the social and economic position of the Indian, who is at the bottom of the social scale. Accordingly, none draws an Indian.

Is it possible that Ladino children cannot draw an Indian? To answer this question we asked a sixth grade Ladino class, in a public school in San Cristobal, which had previously produced 100 per cent Ladino drawings, to draw an Indian. Although upon inquiry it appeared that none had previously drawn an Indian, but all then drew Indians, and their drawings were quite good. The differences between their representations of Ladinos and their representations of Indians were almost solely in terms of dress.

Now let us ask the counterquestion. What types of men are drawn by Zinecanteco and Chamula Indian boys? Many of their homes do not provide pencil and paper, or even a table, and probably for these reasons many of their drawings are very poor. Many drawings by these boys are not classifiable, that is, they cannot be said to represent either Indians or Ladinos. But of those which are classifiable, as shown by Table 2, only 30 per cent represent Indians. In other words, 100 per cent of the classifiable Ladino drawings represent Ladinos, and 70 per cent of the classifiable Indian drawings represent Ladinos.

Our Indian drawings were obtained from Zinecantecos and Chamulas attending primitive rural schools. Fathers of these boys wear native dress. *All of the boys from whom we obtained drawings were in native costume.* Is it possible that they cannot draw the costume they are wearing? After obtaining the results just described, boys in several schools were asked to draw an Indian. Under these instructions, all of their classifiable drawings represented men in Indian costume, usually the costume of their own group.

After we had tested a few Indian schools it was suggested that Indian children were drawing modern men because the directions were given in Spanish. We therefore asked our assistant to give the instructions sometimes in the native language and sometimes in Spanish. No significant differences in results were obtained. If our interpretation is correct, when these Zinecanteco and the Chamula boys are older they will give up native dress. This is a safe prediction because several other groups of Chiapas Indians have already done so. In other words, our results predict for the Chamulas and Zinecantecos what has already happened in other groups.

In third place in Table 2 are the Navaho boys in American Indian schools in 1936. Their drawings are remarkably good. However, only 25 per cent of their classifiable drawings depict Navaho men in the traditional costume which was worn by most Navaho men at that time (see Figure 24). Seventy-five per cent of the classifiable drawings portrayed men in modern costume. We assume that today more Navaho boys would draw men in modern dress. We have not yet tested this prediction but we intend to do so in the near future.

We collected drawings from the Hopi Indians, neighbors of the Navaho, in 1936, but because our collection was lost the Hopi are not included among our main groups. At present we have only a small, recent sample of Hopi drawings from which is provided the illustration of traditional Hopi costume shown in Figure 25. There can be no confusion between it and the Navaho costume.

The Hopi reservation is a small, rectangular tract lying within the much larger Navaho reservation. The Hopis and Navahos are traditional enemies; Navahos formerly raided Hopi villages. The Hopis, who are village people, look down upon the Navahos, most of whom are nomadic and pastoral. Reciprocally, the Navahos look down upon the Hopis. In view of this situation it should be expected, according to our hypothesis, that when Navahos draw Indians they draw only Navahos, and that Hopis draw only Hopis. This is precisely the case.

Yet each group is well acquainted with the appearance of the other. The Navahos trade with the Hopis who are the more sedentary and commercial. In any Hopi village scarcely a day goes by during which Navaho men or Navaho families do not pass through. The Navahos as visitors attend Hopi public ceremonies. That boys in each group, when they draw an Indian, draw only their own traditional dress cannot be explained because of lack of familiarity on the part of one group with the costume of the other group.

Within the United States, besides the Southwestern Indians, there are few groups which today have a traditional style of daily dress. One of these is the Amish, whose costumes vary somewhat according to where they live, Pennsylvania, Ohio, or Iowa. We have drawings only from groups near Lancaster, Pennsylvania, where the men are distinguishable from other Americans on sight because they wear suspenders and broad-rimmed black hats. Pennsylvania Amish boys, when they draw a man, sometimes draw an Amish man as he appears in Figure 26. The Pennsylvania Amish boys attend one-room rural schools located in their own communities and with very few non-Amish children enrolled. All the Amish boys in these schools, which we personally tested, wear Amish costumes. Although they draw some men in Amish costume, the majority of the men are drawn in the modern dress that is not worn by Amish men. Here again a trend toward the abandonment of traditional ways appears to be indicated by drawings.

In some groups, when the folk costume is no longer worn in its entirety, some element or elements of the folk costume persist. Let us begin our discussion of these with the Orthodox, but not Hassidic, boys in Brooklyn who attend Yeshivas (Jewish religious schools). No traditional element of costume is required of them except the skullcap. It is worn at all times at school, and presumably at home (see Figure 27). Nevertheless, only *three* Yeshiva boys in a hundred drew a skullcap. *No* Jewish public school student and no gentile Brooklyn student drew one.

We have indicated that in none of our main groups does traditional dress predominate in its drawings. Let us further document this generalization.

Of the classifiable Israeli Orthodox drawings only 21 per cent represent men whose dress is predominantly traditional. Even fewer nonorthodox Israelis drew traditional dress. In the two Taiwan groups, only 18 per cent in Group I and 11 per cent in Group II drew native dress. Figure 28 illustrates one kind of Taiwan traditional dress. In the Japanese village only 9 per cent of the men drawn are in native costume (see Figure 29), and in Kyoto, only 6 per cent. The remainder of classifiable drawings are modern.

As we have said earlier in connection with Table 2, several groups are not included in Table 2 because for them a native dress does not exist or is used only on special occasions. Within the latter groups, ceremonial dress is seldom drawn. Although kilts still are worn occasionally in Edinburgh, in 400 drawings by Edinburgh boys a man in kilts was represented in only one (see Figure 30). In 70 drawings made by Greek boys in Athens no folk costumes were drawn, although folk costumes are used by palace guards and in parades.

In Lebanon in former times a common article of dress, particularly among the more well-to-do citizens, was a cylindrical, rimless hat with a tassel, called in Arabic a *tarbush* and in Turkish a *fez* (Figure 31). Still often worn in the Lebanese villages, it is less common in Beirut; however, all Beirutis are familiar with it. Tarbushes appear in 30 per cent of the drawings made by boys in three poor Lebanese villages. In the more progressive villages only 16 per cent of the men are drawn with tarbushes, and in the elementary school associated with the American University of Beirut only 8 per cent of the men drawn wear tarbushes. These differences appear to indicate clearly the modernization in attitudes toward dress which have occurred in Lebanon.

If boys who wear traditional dress, such as the Chiapas Indian, the Hassidic, and the Sudanese urban boys, really prefer modern dress, as their drawings seem to show, why do they continue to wear traditional dress?

It must be remembered that boys do not make or buy their own clothes. They cannot wear modern clothes if their parents do not provide them. The reasons that parents do not do so are twofold: the first is that parents may disapprove of modern dress. The second reason is that if parents approve of modern dress, nevertheless they may not have the money to buy modern clothing, nearly all of which is machine-made and must be paid for in currency. Traditional dress is usually homemade, and the adoption of modern dress is made possible only by an increase in income. We predict, on the basis of drawings, that when the standard of living of any group now wearing traditional dress but drawing modern dress improves, modern dress will be worn.

Let us admit again that drawings are not required to make this prediction, because the predicted change has happened already in many groups, and the reverse change has never happened. This is only one instance in which interpretations, based upon drawings, are in accord with other data.

In summary, the data in this chapter indicate that whatever their own dress or the dress of their community, children most often draw the costume which they admire. It is probable that the relative frequencies of modern and traditional dress represent the relative preferences for these two kinds of costumes.

Figure 12   A man in modern dress drawn by a Brooklyn Christian.

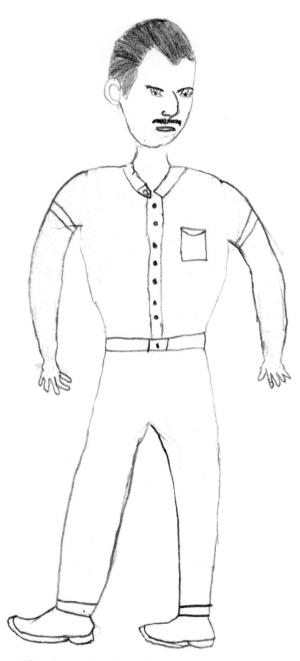

Figure 13   A man in modern dress drawn by a Mexico City boy.

48

Figure 14 A Scot in modern dress.

Figure 15   A Swede in modern dress.

50

Figure 16   An Israeli in modern dress.

Figure 17   A Greek in modern dress.

Figure 18 A Turk in modern dress.

Figure 19   A Beiruti in modern dress.

Figure 20   An Iranian in modern dress.

Figure 21   A Sudanese man in traditional dress.

56

Figure 22   An Hassidic man drawn by a Brooklyn Hassidic boy.

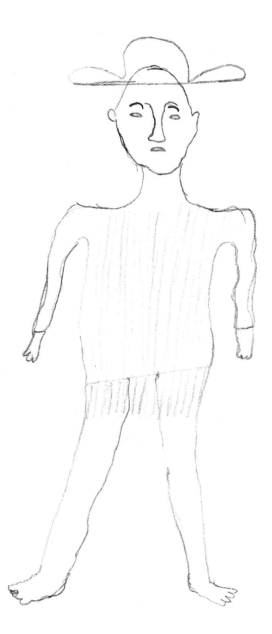

Figure 23 *A Chamula man drawn by a Chamula boy.*

Figure 24   A Navaho man drawn by a Navaho boy.

Figure 25   A Hopi man drawn by a Hopi boy.

60

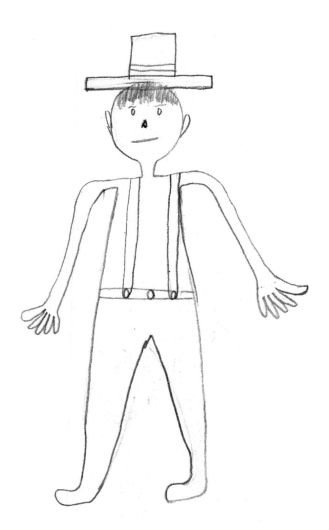

Figure 26   An Amish man drawn by an Amish boy.

Figure 27 A man with a skullcap drawn by a Brooklyn Yeshiva boy.

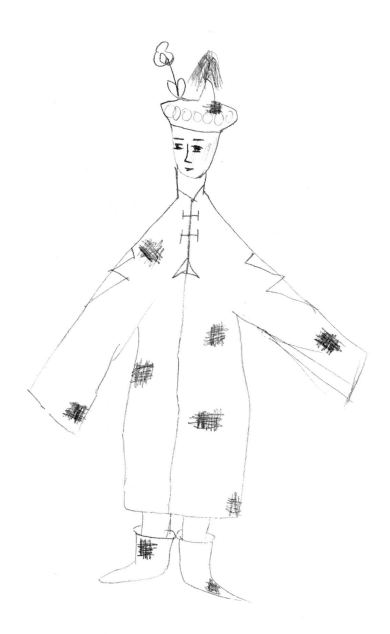

Figure 28   A Chinese man drawn by a Taipei boy.

Figure 29   A Japanese man drawn by a Kyoto boy.

64

Figure 30   The only Scot in kilts in 400 Scottish drawings.

Figure 31   A man with a tarbush drawn by a Lebanese boy.

66

Chapter Five

Physical Features
in Drawings

Some physical features, such as hair color and the straightness or curliness of hair can be changed by frequent use of modern techniques. Others, such as facial conformation, shape of eyes, form of nose and mouth cannot readily be altered. Whether changeable or not, physical features are usually called racial, although it is acknowledged that races are not distinct and that within any "race" there is great variety. However, since we will deal only with certain groups of Caucasians, Orientals, and Negroes, the problem of distinguishing physical features in drawings is simplified.

Drawings by Caucasian Children

No one will be surprised to learn that when children of the white race, whether from North America, Europe, or the Middle East, are asked to draw a man, almost all their drawings represent a white man. Seldom do they draw a man of another group, such as a Japanese man, a Chinese, an Eskimo, or an American Indian. They almost never draw a Negro; of the 1650 white children in our main groups, only one, a German boy, drew a Negro (see Figure 32). As in the case of other exceptional drawings, this *may* have been intended as a caricature.

It has been suggested that when American and European children draw white men the men are white because the children are using white paper. Is this true? We think not. The drawing of a Negro by a German boy (Figure 32) was drawn on white paper, but it clearly represents a Negro, and was labeled as such, even though his skin is not dark. In other words, no group is distinguishable solely on the basis of skin color. The contours of the eyes, nose, chin, and lips, and the appearance of the hair also are involved. If we were to give to white children black paper and white pencils, we have no doubt that most of their drawings would clearly represent members of the white race. Such an experiment should be conducted, but we have not done it.

We present three illustrations which present typical Caucasoid faces; one is by a Swede (Figure 33), one by a Mexican Ladino boy (Figure 34), and one by a Lebanese boy (Figure 35). According to our hypothesis that drawings reflect values, most white children draw white men because the Caucasian believes in his own superiority. The many centuries during which the white man has held a privileged social position in many parts of the world have confirmed him in this belief.

Chinese Drawings

When Marco Polo reached Cathay he found men who felt that they were superior to Caucasians. Marco Polo did not obtain drawings from Chinese children, but had he done so, we believe that the physical features shown in the drawings would have been Chinese. We base this judgment in part upon the fact that Chinese art of that time reflects a preference for Chinese features.

It seems that this feeling persists today. We find that Chinese drawings–recently obtained from Taiwan–show a preference for Oriental features. We analyzed the Taiwan drawings and arranged two categories of facial features represented, the Oriental or the Caucasian. The categorization was based upon slanted versus horizontal eyebrows, narrow versus more rounded opening of the eyes, broad noses versus less broad ones, and round versus elongated faces. The judgment of Oriental or Caucasian was based upon which of the two sets of racial traits predominated. Effort was made not to consider clothing. If a drawing displayed no clear-cut dominance of either Oriental or Caucasian features it was labeled as unclassifiable.

The number of unclassifiable Taipei drawings was large: 44 per cent in Group I and 52 per cent in Group II. This may be due to ambivalence on the part of the Taiwanese. Since the drawings were good, the indeterminate nature of many drawings does not seem to be due to poor skill.

Of the classifiable figures, 84 per cent of Group I and 80 per cent of Group II were judged to have Oriental features. There is a clear-cut predominance of Oriental men. A Taipei child's drawing of an Oriental man is shown in Figure 36, and a Taipei drawing of a Caucasian in Figure 37. Although, like Caucasian groups, the Taiwanese most often draw men of their own physical features, they draw Caucasian features 16 to 20 per cent of the time. In the Caucasian groups the drawing of Orientals is much more rare. We suggest that in Taipei the valuation of Oriental features has decreased from a presumed 100 per cent preference for their own physical features at the time of Marco Polo and may continue to decrease further in the future.

Drawings by Japanese Children

Japanese drawings, like other Oriental drawings, are exceptionally good. One group of Japanese drawings is from Kyoto, a city prominent in history and prominent today. A second group of Japanese drawings was obtained in a mountain village far from any modern city.

Many Japanese drawings, like those from Taipei, reveal their Asiatic origin in the structure of the face. We have applied to the Japanese drawings the same method of categorization which we used with Formosan drawings. The Japanese drawings, however, supply some additional cues as to identity. Frequently, the Japanese boy draws stubbles of facial hair. If he does, the stubbles are only around the mouth, almost never high on the cheeks. This apparently represents a biological difference in appearance between the Orientals and the Caucasians, and perhaps between the Japanese and other Oriental groups.

Being conservative in our categorization, we placed 30 Kyoto drawings in the racially unclassified group; 22 of the Japanese village drawings were so categorized. In the Japanese drawings we found none which to us clearly represents Caucasian men. In other words, 100 per cent of the classifiable drawings represent Japanese, or at least Oriental, men (see Figures 38 and 39). In this connection, it should be noted that a considerable number of Americans have been in Japan since 1946. Despite their familiarity with the appearance of Americans, Japanese children do not draw them. Yet a very large per cent of Japanese men who are drawn wear Western clothes. The attitude represented by the Japanese drawings seems to be: we accept Western technology, but we prefer our own physiognomy.

Drawings from Cambodia

These drawings come from a rural farming village not far from the Cambodian capital of Phnom Penh. Insofar as we can learn it is not an unusual Cambodian village.

Not being familiar with Cambodians at first hand, we can only say that none of the men drawn look to us like Caucasians, nor do they look like the men drawn by the Taiwanese or Japanese. Figure 40 is fairly representative. To treat the various facial traits of Southeast Asia is beyond our competence, but it appears that Cambodians draw men who are not Caucasian, Chinese, or Japanese in respect to physical features. Therefore, they are probably Cambodian.

A Question of Research Technique

A psychologist is aware of the possibility that he may make false judgments in a direction which favors his own theory. Are we prejudiced in thinking that most Caucasian drawings represent Caucasians and that most Asiatic drawings represent Asians?

The sophisticated reader will suggest that we try an objective test. Why not submit to judges a mixed group of drawings made by Caucasian, Taiwanese, Japanese, and Cambodian children, and see whether they can be correctly sorted. We have no doubt that almost anyone can do so, but such a study will be complicated by the presence of secondary cues. In most countries the paper for drawings was obtained locally and differed in thickness and texture from place to place, so that if a sorter were blindfolded, he could classify many drawings correctly by touch. If the sorter were not blindfolded, he could correctly classify many of them merely on the basis of the appearance of the paper.

If the pictures were photographed and reproduced on a uniform kind of paper, most of the Japanese drawings could be identified simply because they are large. The Japanese child is taught that whatever the size of his paper his drawing should occupy most of the space available.

If, by photography, all drawings were made uniform in size, there would still remain differences in drawing tools and techniques which would distinguish many of them. The Cambodian drawings were made with very soft pencils. The Taiwanese children, who use harder pencils, make thinner lines; the Japanese do a great deal of shading. Furthermore, Japanese drawings are usually full-faced. There are only a few profiles in the Japanese drawings, but there are many in the Caucasian and Chinese drawings. The clothing depicted by different groups, even when it is modern, is different. For example, the Japanese add to modern clothing fountain pens, wrist watches, and brief cases, which are seldom drawn by Americans.

In other words, it seems to us impossible to prepare drawings in such a way that judgments as to the origin of the drawings *must* be based on physical features alone. Therefore, in classifying the drawings in reference to physical features we have tried to *attend* to physical features only. We feel that we can do this, but there is no proof that we have succeeded; our hypothesis may have affected our judgment. We would be happy to have others with different hypotheses or different techniques use our materials. Nevertheless, we feel that if, between judges classifying physical features, differences were to be found, these differences would have to be huge to controvert our findings. Among drawings made by Caucasian boys we found almost no drawings of Oriental men; among drawings of Japanese boys almost no Western men. It seems quite unlikely that with the same materials another investigator's judgment would reverse the direction of our findings.

Drawings by American Negroes

No American white child from whom we have obtained a drawing has drawn a Negro. American Negro children also seldom draw a Negro; they draw men nearly all of whom are clearly Caucasian. Figure 41 was drawn by a Negro boy in a rural community in Mississippi, Figure 42, by a Negro boy in Brooklyn. Each is rather typical of the drawings of its group, except that it may be "better" in terms of proficiency.

In addition to the two "main groups" in Mississippi and in Brooklyn, we have also obtained drawings from segregated schools in Maryland and Tennessee and from a Negro university in Washington, D.C. Some of the drawings were obtained by white examiners, some by Negro examiners. Altogether, we have examined more than one thousand drawings made by Negroes who ranged in educational status from Grade 1 to college seniors. Figure 43 shows a man drawn by a Negro university student. In one instance, a Negro university student drew a profile with Negroid features, crossed it out, and drew a more Caucasian profile (Figure 44). These drawings (except Figure 44) have been examined by several psychologists who did not know from what sources they came. They were asked to identify the kind of children who made the drawings. The instructions were very general; race was not mentioned. Only one psychologist correctly guessed their origin; he said they must be drawings made by Negroes because they were so unmistakably *white.*

Control experiments which we have conducted show that when Negro children are asked to draw a Negro they can readily do so, as can white children. To do so they simply darken the exposed skin of the face and hands and change somewhat the facial features and the nature of the hair. Drawings by Sudanese children also show that drawing a Negro presents no problems to children.

Drawings made by Negro children to represent white men show that they can and do use the technique of shading; many of the Mississippi and Brooklyn children, as in Figure 45, shaded one or more areas of their drawings. They used shading in drawing hair, the pupils of the eyes, the eyebrows, or moustache, or clothing, but none used shading to darken the skin.

That the American Negro disapproves of his own facial features has been documented by a large number of studies by social scientists; many of which are summarized by Myrdal in his book *An American Dilemma* (1944). Myrdal shows that American Negroes wish to be light skinned, that within the Negro group light skins are preferred to dark skins, and that light color tends to give a higher social status to its owner. The prevalence of this attitude is demonstrated by the advertisements for skin lotions in Negro magazines. There is a similar emphasis upon "straight" or "good" hair. There is no doubt that if American Negroes could change their features to Caucasian features most of them would do so.

The inescapable conclusion appears to be that Negro children who draw a white man are drawing the appearance which they would like to possess. This does not necessarily mean that they like other aspects of a white man aside from his appearance. They may be resentful of the treatment which they have received from white people, but they would like to look like them and to have their social position.

In Africa, before the advent of the white man, many African carvings and cave paintings of men were done in black and had Negroid features. However, at that historical period Negroes may have depicted Negroes because white men were unknown to them, not because of racial pride. Were Negro children today to possess pride in their own race and heritage, we assume that they would draw Negroes. But the present technological, military, and educational status of the white nations in comparison with the Negro nations makes it seem likely that few Negro children, even in Africa, possess such pride. Whether or not this deduction is correct would be very interesting and important to determine. We do not have adequate evidence on this point, but, as we have noted earlier, drawings from Sudan obtained by Dr. Malik Badri show that *some* Sudanese Negro children draw Negroes. Figure 46 was obtained in a Sudanese village. The number of Sudanese village drawings which we have seen is not great enough to show the accurate proportion of village children who draw Negroes, but, of the total Sudanese drawings collected by Dr. Badri, the majority represent white men.

In summary, in this chapter we have seen that Caucasian children almost always draw men of their own race, and that children in Taiwan, Japan, and Cambodia also most often draw men with their own physical features. On the other hand, American Negroes nearly always draw Caucasians, not Negroes or Orientals. The facts presented in this chapter appear to be consonant with the theory that, whatever their own race, children draw men who have the physical features which they admire. As we suggested in the case of costume, so it may be in regard to race, that in any group the proportion of drawings representing each of the several races will represent the relative preferences for the physical features of various racial groups.

The two main Negro groups were tested in 1962. It is possible that in some areas Negro attitudes have undergone change since that time.

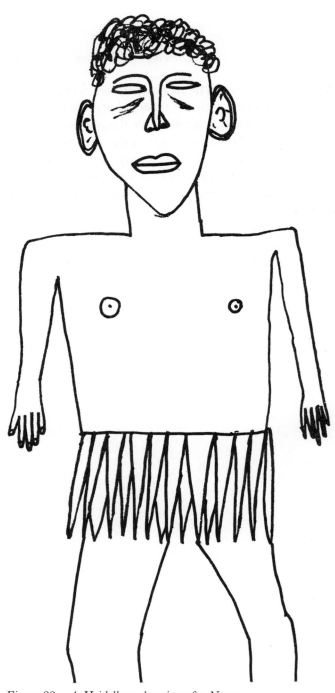

Figure 32   A Heidelberg drawing of a Negro.

Figure 33   A Swedish drawing of a Caucasian.

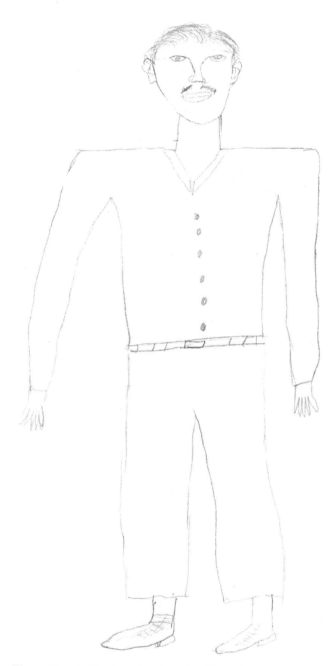

Figure 34   A Mexican drawing of a Caucasian.

Figure 35   A Lebanese drawing of a Caucasian.

Figure 36   A Taiwanese man drawn by a Taipei boy.

Figure 37   A Caucasian drawn by a Taipei boy.

81

Figure 38   A Japanese drawn by a Kyoto boy.

82

Figure 39   A Japanese drawn by a Japanese village boy.

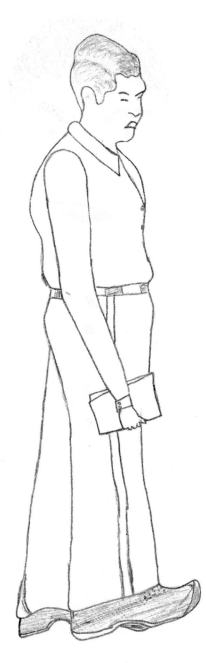

Figure 40   A Cambodian man drawn by a Cambodian boy.

84

Figure 41   A Caucasian drawn by a Mississippi Negro boy.

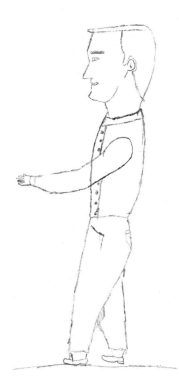

Figure 42   A Caucasian drawn by a Brooklyn Negro boy.

86

Figure 43   A Caucasian drawn by a Negro university student.

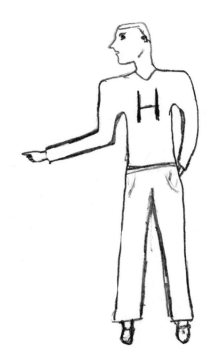

Figure 44   A changed drawing made by a Negro university student.

Figure 45   A drawing with shading made by a Mississippi Negro boy.

Figure 46   A Negro man drawn by a Sudanese boy.

Chapter Six

Emphasis on Masculinity

There are large differences among groups in respect to the frequencies with which boys draw men with moustaches; this is also true of their representation of beards and facial stubble. Similarly, groups of boys vary in respect to the number of men drawn smoking cigars or pipes, the number with unrealistically broad shoulders, and in the number dressed for various masculine occupations, such as the policeman or the athlete. A fifth category refers to the depicting of men carrying canes or weapons.

In almost all societies the aspects of appearance which have just been cited emphasize the distinction between men and women. Table 3 compares the frequencies of the items described above in four groups chosen because they differed considerably in the frequencies of these items. These groups consist of boys from Heidelberg, boys from Mexico City, Brooklyn white Christians, and Chiapas Indians.

If one reads downward in Table 3, one finds that except for two slight inversions there is a consistent decrease in the

Table 3   Frequencies of Certain Items in the Drawings of Four Groups

Group	Facial hair	Pipes or cigars	Shoulder emphasis	Masculine costume	Canes or weapons
Heidelberg	30	35	10	32	28
Mexico City	19	5	18	23	5
Brooklyn white Christians	8	6	7	10	1
Chiapas Indians	3	0	0	1	0

incidence of each of these items, that is, the occurrences of these items are related among these groups. This is also true if twenty-seven groups are compared, rather than four.

Because these masculine traits are associated with each other, we appear to be justified in utilizing them to derive a rating of masculinity of appearance. This can be done in two ways: either by counting the number of drawings in each group which has one or more items of masculine emphasis, or by counting the number of masculine items in each drawing and obtaining a mean. We have chosen to use the first method, for two reasons. One is that it is more conservative, that is, the group differences in scores derived from this method are smaller. Secondly, it obviates the criticism that some items of masculine emphasis, such as canes or football uniforms, are present in some cultures but not in others. In other words, it seems best to score a drawing as masculine if it has one or more items of masculine emphasis in terms of the culture from which it comes. We have not included military uniforms in our indices of masculinity, although occasionally we will refer to the incidence of drawings of modern military men. One reason for not including them is that in some groups, specifically the Germans and the Japanese, there appears today to be a taboo upon the representation of modern military personnel.

Table 4 shows the per cent of drawings in each group which contain one or more items of masculine emphasis. In one group, the Heidelberg boys, 71 per cent of the drawings have one or more items of masculine emphasis. Of these, Figure 47 provides an illustration. After Heidelberg, Taipei I, Gothenburg, and Mexico City follow, in that order (see Figures 48, 49, 50). Below these high-rating groups, many other groups follow closely. The three lowest groups are boys from Lebanese villages Group II, Brooklyn Yeshiva boys, and the Chiapas Indians (see Figures 51, 52, 53). The contrast in appearance between the high masculinity and low masculinity drawings is marked.

We believe that the hypothesis that differences in drawings between the high ranking and low ranking groups reflect differences in values in respect to masculinity could be validated in detail by historical and other social science data, although such validation is beyond the scope of the present project.

In view of the high score obtained in Heidelberg, we regret that we do not have other German data. We cannot conclude from this set of drawings that there is a masculinity emphasis among Germans in general. However, relevant

Table 4   Per Cents of Drawings Showing Masculine Emphasis

71	Heidelberg	36	
*		35	
*		34	
*		33	
59	Taipei I	32	
58		31	
57		30	Cambodia
56		29	
55		28	Brooklyn Hassidim
54		27	Brooklyn Negroes
53	Gothenburg	26	Israeli nonorthodox
52		25	Mississippi Negroes
51		24	Lebanese villages I
50	Mexico City	23	Brooklyn public school Jews
49		22	Ankara
48		21	
47	Kyoto	20	Israeli Orthodox
46	Taipei II	19	
45	Armenian Lebanese	18	Brooklyn white Christians
44	Japanese village	17	Tehran
43	Edinburgh	16	
42		15	Lebanese villages II
41	Athens	14	Brooklyn Yeshivas
40	Navahos	*	
39	Beirut	*	
38		*	
37	San Cristobal	3	Chiapas

facts come to mind in respect to the history of the Gemanic peoples. Their mythology has a strong masculine emphasis, as does their history. They played an important part in balking the expansion of the Roman Empire and in its overthrow. Appeals to strength, courage, militancy, and superiority were used effectively in World War I and World War II. Despite these factors, the Germans were defeated in both wars. Thus, it is interesting to note that few Heidelberg drawings, despite their general masculinity, depict men in modern military uniform. Depictions of ancient men of war occur in Heidelberg drawings to a degree not seen in any other group (see as an example Figure 54). Not only portraits of ancient European warriors are drawn, but also pictures of American Indian warriors (Figure 55). It is possible that the tradition of the German as a warrior, while presently curbed, is shown indirectly in these pictures. The high Heidelberg score in respect to masculine emphasis is earned in other ways, in addition to the representation of warriors. Thirty-five per cent of the men drawn by Heidelberg boys are smoking pipes; 30 per cent carry weapons. The Heidelberg masculine emphasis is general.

In the case of Taipei, we are acquainted with few literary and cultural data which might show that the high emphasis upon masculinity is historically based. It is worthy of note, however, that in contrast to the Germans, who were forbidden to rearm for a period after World War II and do not draw modern military men, the Taiwanese have been encouraged to arm themselves. Perhaps as a consequence Taiwan boys draw men of whom 16 per cent are modern soldiers. In this respect, their score exceeds that of all other groups. As we have noted previously these percentages do not contribute to the masculinity scores shown in Table 4, because modern military uniforms were not included in our indices of masculine emphasis; however, this finding supports the findings represented in Table 4. If 16 per cent were added to the Taipei masculinity scores, they would not be significantly lower than the Heidelberg group.

The Chiapas Indians are significantly below all other groups in respect to masculine emphasis. Only three of their drawings were scored as exhibiting a masculine emphasis. One Chiapas man was classified as showing masculine emphasis because he had a knife in his belt, one because he carried a planting stick (which women do not carry), and one because he wore a moustache.

The lack of masculine traits among Chiapas Indian drawings may be due in some degree to poor drawing skill. However, these boys were *in school* and hence represented a high academic group among their people. Furthermore, among the Chiapas boys who remain in school to age eleven or above, performance in drawing is not bad. Still, not much skill seems to be required to include in a drawing some of the indicators of masculinity, such as a moustache, a pipe, a cigar, wide shoulders, a knife, or a gun, and these were seldom drawn.

That the Chiapas Indian drawings are nonmasculine is probably due to the social structure of the society in which they live. As described previously, they are subservient to the Ladinos. If they are aggressive toward Ladinos, they are jailed. Although there is no law prohibiting their carrying of weapons, for an Indian to do so would be greatly resented by the Ladinos. There is no law in Chiapas that an Indian cannot wear a moustache, but since many Ladinos wear moustaches the wearing of moustaches is thought of as a Ladino prerogative. The same is true of the smoking of pipes or cigars. In other words, the almost total absence of indices of masculinity in the drawings of Chiapas Indian boys is probably due to the inhibiting influence of the dominant Ladino culture.

In contrast to the scarcity of masculine symbols in Indian drawings in Chiapas, such symbols are present in 37 per cent of the drawings of Ladino boys of San Cristobal. This value is lower than the 50 per cent which occurs in Mexico City, but both values are relatively high and are in accord with the tradition that in Mexico a Ladino must be "muy macho," that is, very masculine.

In brief, the evidence presented in this chapter tends to show that in groups which stress the importance of masculinity, distinctively masculine traits appear in the drawings of boys more often than they do in the drawings of groups in which masculinity is not stressed, or in which its visible expression is inhibited.

Figure 47   A man with masculine emphasis drawn by a Heidelberg boy.

Figure 48   A man with masculine emphasis drawn by a Taipei boy.

Figure 49   A man with masculine emphasis drawn by a Gothenberg boy.

Figure 50   A man with masculine emphasis drawn by a Mexican boy.

100

Figure 51   A man without masculine emphasis drawn by a Lebanese boy.

*Figure 52   A man without masculine emphasis
drawn by a Brooklyn Yeshiva boy.*

102

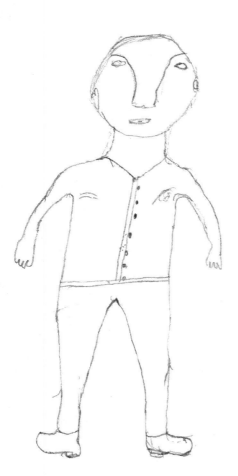

Figure 53   *A man without masculine emphasis*
drawn by a Zinecanteco Indian boy.

103

Figure 54   A medieval warrior drawn by a German boy.

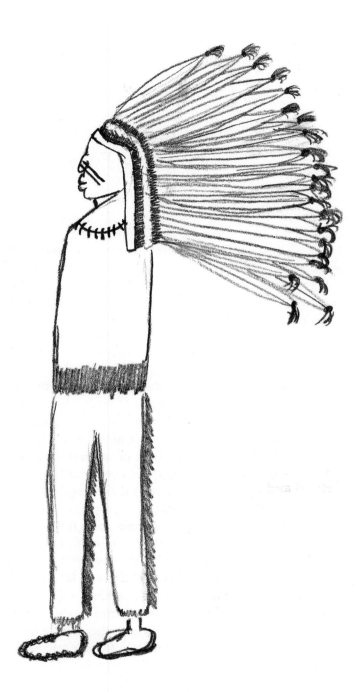

Figure 55   *An American Indian drawn by a German boy.*

Chapter Seven

Smiling and
Nonsmiling Faces

The greatest differences among groups
were found in the frequencies of smiling faces drawn. Inci-
dences of smiling men in drawings by boys can be as much as
75 or as little as 4 per cent. What is the proper interpretation
of such variation in the occurrence of smiling in drawings?
Before attempting to interpret the meaning of the smile in
children's drawings, we must first indicate our criteria for a
smile.

At the beginning of our study of smiling, we asked an
assistant to indicate whether each of many drawings did or
did not represent a smiling face. We soon found that this re-
sulted in low agreement between us and our assistant. In discussions it appeared that the two of us were responding in
different degrees to the mouth, the eyes, and to lines on the
forehead and cheeks. In children's drawings these aspects of
appearance are often in conflict.

To improve the objectivity of judgments it was decided to
base judgments of smiling upon the mouth alone. The rule
was that for a face to be scored as smiling, both corners of the
mouth must turn upward. When the mouth is represented by
a single line, or when the closed lips form a single line, the
rule applies to these lines; if the mouth is open, it applies to
the upper lip. With such a definition the scoring agreement
between two judges was better than 90 per cent. All of the
data presented were scored by these rules. Table 5 shows
the per cents of smiling faces among different groups. Many

of the differences shown in Table 5 are highly significant, although differences between adjacent groups usually are not significant.

The reader will remember that we have included in each table only "main groups." Primarily they are groups in which the number of drawings obtained from a school or from a community totaled one hundred. It seems important to note that several small samples of American drawings exhibit smiling frequencies appreciably greater than the highest shown in Table 5. They consist of the following: public school children in a suburban group in a Long Island school, in Amish rural schools near Lancaster, Pennsylvania, in Larned, Kansas, and in Rockville, Maryland. These groups

Table 5   Numbers of Drawings Portraying Smiles

59	Brooklyn white Christians	25	
*		24	Taipei II
*		23	
*		22	Kyoto
43	Brooklyn public school Jews	21	Cambodia
42	Brooklyn Yeshiva boys	20	Mexico City
41	Brooklyn Hassidim	19	
40		18	Heidelberg
39		17	
38		16	
37	nonorthodox Israelis	15	
36		14	Navahos
35	Gothenburg	13	
34		12	San Cristobal
33	Brooklyn Negroes	11	Beirut
32		10	Ankara
31	Japanese village	9	Tehran, Armenian Lebanese
30		8	Mississippi Negroes
29	Taipei I	7	Orthodox Israelis, Athens,
28			Lebanese villages I
27	Edinburgh	6	
26		5	Chiapas Indians
		4	Lebanese villages II

have in common the fact that each consists almost wholly of white Christians whose ancestors have been in the United States for several generations and have been called "Old Americans." When combined they total one hundred and their incidence of smiling is 75 per cent. (For an example see Figure 56.) This incidence of smiling is significantly higher than the 59 per cent found among white Christians in Brooklyn. In general Brooklyn white Christians consist of families who came to the United States more recently than the "Old Americans." Three Brooklyn Jewish groups who are children of relatively recent immigrants from Europe scored 43, 42, and 41 per cent.

Groups in Northern Europe and certain other groups outside of the United States who are of European derivation score somewhat lower than recently arrived American groups. They are nonorthodox Israelis (from Europe), 37 per cent; Gothenberg, 35 per cent; Edinburgh, 27 per cent; Mexico City, 20 per cent; and Heidelberg, 18 per cent. Figure 57 shows a Scot, who, under great provocation, is smiling. Middle Eastern groups score lower still: Beirut, 11 per cent; Ankara, 10 per cent; and Tehran, 9 per cent. Orthodox Israelis from the Middle East, Athenians, and Lebanese villages I are very low (7 per cent). The primitive Chiapas Indians and the least modernized Lebanese villages score lowest (5 and 4 per cent, respectively).

In other words, among these groups there is a gradient extending from the Old Americans of European descent, through groups presently living in Northern Europe and Israelis of relatively recent European ancestry, to persons who have only begun to be "Westernized." As we have noted, the range of scores in these groups is between 75 and 4 per cent.

We suggest that the explanation for this scale of smiling frequencies is a cultural one, having to do with the relative importance of hedonism as a goal. Within the past two centuries the idea that earthly happiness is one of man's chief goals has developed rapidly in America. Only in the United States has it been officially declared (in the Declaration of Independence) that the pursuit of happiness is one of the inalienable rights of man. Those children whose families have been in America for more than a century seem to have absorbed this idea, and they reflect it in their drawings. To Europeans, and to families more recently from Europe, it appears that hedonism is not so strong a goal as it is to Old Americans. Happiness is only now becoming a dominant goal among Middle Eastern peoples.

In other words, it is our interpretation that the drawing of smiling faces reflects the extent to which to have a smiling face is a social goal. We believe that happiness, and the expression of it, is most highly rated in Old American groups, next by European groups and groups recently from Europe, and is rated least in the Middle Eastern groups and among those who share only slightly the "Western" tradition. Those groups which lie outside this tradition will be treated later.

It is necessary to emphasize that the present emphasis upon hedonism in Western society is relatively new. Europeans coming to America brought with them a dour view of life. The Puritans who came to New England in 1620 pictured life as a precarious and serious affair, even for children. Children should fear God, respect their elders and not have fun. By a series of social changes which we cannot here attempt to trace, this doctrine has changed in the United States so that now the American child has a right to enjoyment and almost an obligation to achieve it, and his face should show that happiness is being achieved. In line with this interpretation is the idea that one should smile when greeted and when having one's picture taken. Following this attitude, American advertisements are based on the premise that if one buys the right car, eats the right foods, drinks the right drinks, he will smile. This simple principle is learned early in

America. Drawings by American children of four and five years, not presented here, show that they comprehend it. Smiling faces in drawings are as frequent at these ages as at later ages.

It would appear that in Northern Europe the change from other philosophies of life to hedonism has occurred more slowly, and in Mediterranean and Middle Eastern countries more slowly still. In these countries the values of dignity, family pride, seriousness, obedience, respect to elders are still impressed upon the child. Their drawings express this.

At this point, the smiling frequencies of non-Western groups and of American Negro groups need to be discussed. In general the Eastern Asiatic values lie between the high and low Caucasian percentages to which we have given our attention. The proportions of smiling faces in Asian groups are as follows: a Japanese village, 31 per cent (see Figure 58); Taipei I, 29 per cent; Taipei II, 24 per cent; Kyoto, 22 per cent; a Cambodian village, 21 per cent. Most of these groups do not differ significantly from each other but do differ significantly from several higher and lower groups. We are unable at present to suggest why these Asiatic groups occupy the relatively uniform position which they hold. It appears obvious, however, that the expression of a hedonistic goal is not high among them.

American Negroes are historically "Old Americans" but they have not shared much of the American tradition. When they came as slaves their social role was to serve the white man, and basically this role has not changed. To be happy (and therefore to look happy) is not a feasible role for many Negroes today. The low frequencies of smiles in Negro drawings are in accord with this hypothesis. In the Brooklyn Negro group, only 33 per cent of the men drawn have smiling faces; in the Mississippi group, 8 per cent (see Figure 59). This places the Brooklyn Negro group with the Europeans and the Mississippi group with the Middle Easterners in respect to the incidence of smiling faces in drawings made by each group.

That the American Negro drawings are lower than those of American whites in frequencies of smiles may have causes other than those mentioned previously. Among Negroes of the lower class to which many American Negroes belong, it is likely that the attention given by adults to children and the attempt by adults to provide them with interesting and entertaining activities are considerably less than among whites. It is possible that the underpriviledged Negro child is actually encouraged *not* to expect pleasure by frequently being reminded of his inferior social and economic position. The attitude that happiness for a Negro is a nonattainable goal at present may be communicated by many Negroes to their children.

Let us now consider the incidence of smiling in American Indian drawings (Navahos, 14 per cent; Chiapas Indians, 5 per cent). We may note that dignity and seriousness in the presence of others are emphasized by southwestern United States Indians and Mexican Indians. In short, none of our findings in respect to smiling seem to offer difficulty to the interpretation that smiling faces are most often drawn by groups among whom to have a smiling face is a valued goal. However, several alternative interpretations are possible and must be considered. One of these is that in drawing smiling and nonsmiling faces children draw what they see. This is our friend, the familiarity hypothesis which claims that drawings reflect "real life."

We have not systematically gathered data on the actual frequency of smiling in various groups. We should do so because at present we can give only anecdotal evidence. We ride the subways and buses of New York, as do many white Christian boys and Jewish boys who are listed at the top of Table 5. Anyone who has shared our transportation experiences will not claim that Americans smile while enjoying urban transportation, and observations supporting the view that Americans seldom smile could be made on the street or in the classroom, as well as in the subway.

Another possibility is that boys who draw smiling faces are boys who themselves are happy, that is, that euphoria leads to smiling and that smiling leads to the drawing of smiling. Of course, if boys who draw smiling faces seldom smile, as we have proposed, this chain of reasoning breaks down. Obviously we need more data. If the gathering of the drawings which we are discussing had not occupied us for several years, we would be tempted to assemble more information before completing this page. It seems better to communicate the data which we now have and to hope that younger men will challenge us, or come to our aid. Meanwhile, we are convinced that facial expression in drawings has little to do with the pleasant or unpleasant state of mind of the artist while he is drawing, or at other times, but rather that it has to do with the vision of what men should be.

Let us introduce some additional anecdotal evidence on this point. Chiapas Indian boys put smiles on the faces of only 5 per cent of their drawings of men. In San Cristobal, Mexico, we lived in a house, the windows of which (because of the relative intensities of inside and outside lighting) provided almost the equivalent of a one-way screen. Many Chiapas Indians after selling and buying in San Cristobal stopped opposite our window to rest and have lunch, not knowing they were being observed. In this setting, smiling was frequently observed, but when one sees Chiapas Indians on the street, smiling is infrequent, as it is in their drawings. This observation tends to show that in respect to smiling versus nonsmiling drawings we are dealing with approved public behavior, not with private behavior.

Another interpretation to be considered is that smiling in drawings reflects the standard of living, that is, a smiling man is a prosperous one. Many of the percentages in Table 5 can be interpreted in this way. The high-percentage groups tend to be those with high income; the low-percentage groups in many cases have low incomes.

However, there are many exceptions to this rule. The Old Americans in Brooklyn with a high incidence of smiling, although not poor, have modest incomes. The Gothenburg, Edinburgh, and Heidelberg groups, who score much lower in smiling, are certainly as high in socioeconomic status as the Old Americans groups from which we obtained drawings. The higher social class groups in Mexico City, Athens, and Beirut are definitely more prosperous than several American groups, but among the former smiles in drawings are much less frequent than among the latter.

Technological advances have been great in Heidelberg, Mexico City, and Beirut, but these cities appear not yet to have accepted a smiling man as a goal image. On the whole, our prediction is that when a high standard of living is attained and maintained in a group, the incidence of smiling faces in drawings may increase. However, such a change appears to depend not upon prosperity per se but upon the acceptance of an ideology; smiling is not an automatic accompaniment of modern technology.

To us, the data in this chapter show that under the conditions in which our drawings were obtained children draw men with smiling faces in proportion to the degree to which smiling is socially approved.

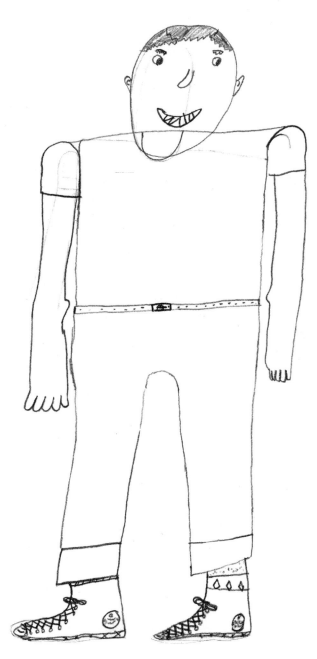

Figure 56   A smiling man drawn by an American white Christian.

Figure 57 A smiling Scot.

Figure 58   A smiling Japanese.

116

Figure 59   A nonsmiling Mississippi Negro drawing.

Chapter Eight

The Infrequency
of Work

When one examines hundreds of drawings made by boys of eleven, twelve, and thirteen years of age, one wonders how the world's work gets done, or perhaps we should say that one wonders how it will get done by the next generation.

A research assistant went through most of the main groups of drawings and was instructed to count each drawing which portrayed a man who was working, was in workman's clothing, or was in an occupational setting, whether as a garbage man, a street cleaner, a farmer, a bookkeeper, a banker, or a doctor, in other words, to count every man who appeared to be gainfully employed in whatever manner. According to our instructions, a man drawn holding a shovel, or sitting behind a desk, or wearing a stethoscope was to be counted as being at work, whether busy or not. In most groups, according to our assistant's count, the number of men at work was not far from zero. Thinking there must have been some misunderstanding, we repeated the count and obtained almost exactly the same results.

The final results obtained are represented in Table 6; names of groups with zero scores have been omitted in order to simplify the table. In all, Table 6 shows that only 50 out of 2550 drawings, or approximately 2 per cent, represented men as presumably working.

The highest proportion of men drawn as working was found in a relatively poor Edinburgh neighborhood. In a sample of 100 Edinburgh drawings one man holds a trowel, one a rake, one a shovel; one is a gas station attendant; one is painting a house; one wears overalls; two are carrying lunch boxes. Two hold microphones; five carry brief cases, but they appear to be students rather than businessmen. If we are conservative and do not count the latter, there are in this group ten men in one hundred who may be presumed to be engaged in gainful occupations. For the Scots, this figure is scandalous. Figure 60 shows one Scotsman who is at work.

The Cambodian drawings are second to Edinburgh in the depiction of work. Nine of the one hundred men drawn are at work or are dressed for work, mostly agricultural: but, in fact, nearly 100 per cent of the men of the Cambodian village are so employed. Figure 61 represents a Cambodian agricultural worker.

Only eight men were drawn as working in a relatively isolated Japanese mountain village. Figure 62 is representative of these drawings.

In brief, the highest percentages of men gainfully employed which we have found in boys' drawings lie between 8 and 10 per cent. This is not to deny that groups might be found with higher percentages, but it should be noted that some of the groups from which our data come are renowned for their industriousness.

Let us now review the record of some of the groups in

Table 6   The Per Cent of Men in Each Group Portrayed as Working

10	Edinburgh
9	Cambodia
8	Japanese village
7	
6	Armenian Lebanese
5	Kyoto
4	
3	Taipei I
2	San Cristobal, Taipei II, Heidelberg
1	Ankara, Athens, Israeli nonorthodox, Brooklyn Yeshivas, Tehran

which even fewer workers are drawn. In the drawings made by one hundred Brooklyn white Christian boys, none is portrayed as working, or in occupational dress, or in a work setting. Likewise, the Jewish boys in Brooklyn public schools drew no man who was working. No Brooklyn Negro boy drew a man who appeared to be gainfully employed. Who works in Brooklyn? Almost everyone does, but children's drawings do not show it.

In 100 German drawings, only two men were at work, and one of them appears not to be working hard (see Figure 63). Among drawings by 100 Turkish students only one man was working. Table 6 shows that only one man or no man was working in each of the other groups. Children's drawings appear to indicate that total unemployment is almost universal and that the next generation is well prepared for the effects of automation.

How is one to understand the infrequency of work in children's drawings? In searching for the explanation of the infrequency of working men in drawings, we are reminded that there exists in every society a hierarchy of occupational status. The order of this hierarchy differs somewhat from one society to another, but in general, professional and managerial men rank high, and unskilled occupations requiring little education rank low in social position. The idea therefore occurs that few workers are represented in drawings because workers have low prestige, that is, they are not goal figures.

This would be explanatory if we had defined workers as manual laborers. If the reader has read carefully he will remember that this was not the case. If a person had been standing near a cash register, or standing in a teller's box, or beside a ticket box, he would have been scored as being at work, but there were no such drawings. Nonwork drawings frequently portray men in recognizable settings, but they are not places of work; Figure 64 provides a Japanese example.

Another possible explanation of our results is that children's drawings seldom show men engaged in *any* form of activity. With some groups who draw poorly, this is true, but several of our groups frequently represent men in action. In terms of drawing proficiency the Heidelberg and Kyoto groups are probably the best. Although few children in these groups draw men at work, they frequently show men engaged in other activities. Among the Kyoto drawings, one man is holding a camera (Figure 65); another one is going to or coming from a bath (Figure 66). The Heidelberg drawings show that German boys can draw men engaged in or prepared for activities. One is riding a horse (see Figure 67), four are reading newspapers (Figure 68 shows one of these), thirty-five are smoking. Eleven German pictures represent cowboys, Indians, or gunmen, and there are seven Greek, Roman or medieval warriors. This is not a complete catalog of the recognizable men of action drawn by Heidelberg boys but those just itemized total fifty-nine nonworking men, in comparison with two workers in the German group. Emphasis has been placed upon the contents of the Kyoto and the Heidelberg drawings both because they are excellent and because the Japanese and the Germans each have a reputation for industriousness. They draw men in varied costumes and activities, but seldom men in occupational activities.

One final explanation of the infrequency of work in drawings is that young boys, although acquainted with men's sports and recreations, are not acquainted with the work activities of men. Fathers are rarely seen at work by their children. Their places of work and their activities are distant from their homes.

It is true that some occupational activities have a low degree of visibility to children. For example, it is difficult to explain to a child, and to others, what a mathematician or a theoretical physicist does. However, ignorance of such esoteric activities provides only a small part of the explanation of the absence of useful activities in drawings. All the boys from whom drawings were obtained were in school. Many came to school in buses, but bus drivers were seldom drawn. All boys had haircuts, but no barber was drawn. Policemen were on duty near the schools, yet were seldom represented. Most boys between ages eleven and thirteen have been examined by a doctor or a dentist, but in boys' drawings one does not see these men.

The truth seems to be that boys of these ages are not interested in and do not value work activities. Our drawings, however, were obtained chiefly in academic schools where little of what is taught is aimed at occupational involvement, but the detachment of schools from everyday life aside, it may be that from a boy's point of view work is something which will concern him only at a vague future date. The problem may be deeper and involve the fact that when a boy begins to work, it is often not because he wishes to do so. For many adults, work is an unfortunate necessity, not a source of status or achievement. Adults, if asked to draw a man, also may seldom draw a man at work. Many persons do not find their work engrossing. In short, the principle that persons draw what they admire and aspire to is not contradicted by the findings that boys seldom draw occupational activities. This finding points to a problem which faces not merely boys, but also men.

Figure 60   A Scottish laborer.

Figure 61   A Cambodian farmer.

Figure 62   A Japanese worker.

Figure 63   A German sailor.

126

Figure 64   A Japanese nonworker.

Figure 65   A Japanese with a camera.

128

Figure 66   To or from the bath (Japanese).

Figure 67   An equestrian (German).

Figure 68   A newspaper reader (German).

131

Chapter Nine

The Religious Content
of Drawings

If the absence of work in drawings is conspicuous, the absence of religious content is more so. Our main groups represent many religions. Several of our American groups and all the Mexican and European groups are Christian. Three American groups and two Israeli groups are Jewish. The Turks, the Iranians, and half of the Lebanese are Moslems; the Cambodians and some of the Japanese are Buddhists.

For each of these groups there exists the possibility of representing religious men in their drawings. Each group has professional religious men: clergymen, priests, rabbis, mullahs, or monks, who wear distinctive costumes. Each group has a traditional posture for prayer. Some groups have religious insignia, such as the Christian cross or the Jewish Star of David. Each group has a recognizable place of worship, such as a church, a synogogue, a temple, or a mosque, in which or in front of which a man could be drawn to show that he is engaged or is about to be engaged in religious rituals or worship.

Notwithstanding these apparently rich opportunities to portray religious activities and settings, little religious content is present in the drawings of any group, except those of the Hassidim. The Hassidic man wears curls before his ears, a broad-rimmed hat, and a full beard. One or more of these items of appearance were drawn by 29 per cent of our Brooklyn Hassidic subjects, and by 22 per cent of the Israeli

Orthodox boys, some of whom were Hassidic. However, such drawings are ambiguous in respect to interpretation, just as the suspenders of the Amish are ambiguous. The Hassidim and the Amish are religious groups, but they are also ethnic groups. The characteristic costume of a group may indicate group membership without necessarily indicating a religious interest. It may show approval of group membership without showing a concern with religious principles or a desire to participate in worship. Among the drawings of two hundred American Jewish boys, both Yeshiva and Hassidic, only one drawing shows a man engaged in a religious *activity* (see Figure 69), and no man is placed in a religious setting. It seems best therefore to assume that aspects of appearance, such as the Hassidic *payes,* or earcurls, represent conformity to ethnic tradition rather than a religious attitude.

Although an ethnic costume may or may not also be religious, whether or not a drawing represents a member of the clergy, or a monastic order or an historical religious figure may be rather objectively determined. In these categories we find only six figures in all of the drawings. In 400 Scottish drawings, one Scottish boy drew a monk (Figure 70), and another drew a priest (Figure 71). An Armenian Lebanese made a drawing possibly intended to be Moses (Figure 72). Another Lebanese boy drew a figure, possibly of a saint or of a crusader (Figure 73). Among three hundred Mexican boys, one drew Morelos, who was not only a priest but also a reformer and political leader (Figure 74). With Figure 69 this list comprises a total of six persons in more than 2500 drawings.

No boy drew a man who was praying; no place of worship or shrine, was drawn as the setting for a human figure. No baptismal rites, confirmation rites, marriage rites, or other religious services were depicted.

To pursue this matter a bit further, we review the fact that the wearing of skullcaps is compulsory in Yeshivas and is considered a religious requirement, rather than merely a group custom. Yet only three in one hundred Brookyln Yeshiva boys drew skullcaps, although all wear them. Eighteen other Yeshiva boys drew hats. That boys who are compelled by religious custom to wear headgear seldom draw headgear can be interpreted as a rejection of a compulsory religious practice on the part of many.

Many groups of Gentile boys drew men with hats more frequently than did the Yeshiva students. Seventy-two per cent of the Navaho boys drew hats; 61 per cent of the Heidelberg boys and 43 per cent of the Chiapas Indians drew men with hats. In none of these groups is the wearing of hats a religious obligation; it is merely a social tradition.

In all, these data suggest that few eleven-, twelve-, and thirteen-year-olds show concern with religious men, religious places, religious activities. This need not show an antireligious sentiment but indicates that a deep positive interest in religion is infrequent, except perhaps on the part of Hassidic boys.

Figure 69   The only Jewish drawing representing a religious activity.

Figure 70   The only monk drawn by a Scot.

136

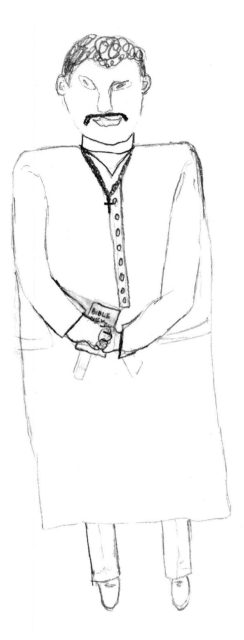

Figure 71   The only other religious figure drawn by a Scot.

Figure 72   *The only religious figure drawn by an Armenian Lebanese.*

138

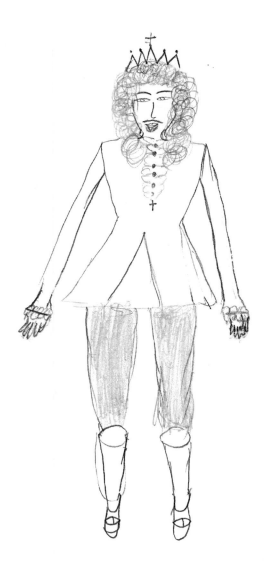

Figure 73   The only religious figure drawn by a Lebanese Arab.

Figure 74   The only religious figure drawn by a Mexican boy.

140

Chapter Ten

The Diversity of
Social Roles

We have seen that the majority of drawings in each of the main groups represent men in modern dress, that the racial variation in each group is small, and that few drawings in any group represent men at work or engaged in religious activities. It can be deduced from these findings that in many groups few drawings have distinctive content.

In general this is true. Boys in many groups draw men who are well dressed, standing, facing the viewer, perhaps smiling, but doing little else. However, the drawings of some groups are quite diversified in respect to the kinds of men drawn. By diversified figures we refer to such men of special types identified by specific clothing or activities, such as swimmers, skiers, fishermen, hunters, tourists, clowns, foreigners, cowboys, gunmen, sheriffs, ancient warriors, readers, hikers, spacemen, farmers, and teachers as contrasted to nondistinctive men in street dress or generalized human figures.

In this chapter we will deal with the results of placing each drawing made by the twenty-seven main groups into one of two categories. One of these we will call standard men; the second consists of diversified men. In the first category is placed any drawing which represents a generalized human being not clearly belonging to any group and any drawing of a man who is distinguished only by wearing modern dress or the traditional dress of his society. All other drawings are

141

said to represent diversified social roles. The percentage of the latter in any group of drawings may be said to represent the degree of differentiation of drawings in that group or the degree of individuality among the drawings of the group. As we use the term, a monk, a carpenter, a doctor is a diversified figure because he is distinguishable from the other men who are drawn. We have not included a drawing in the diversified category merely because the man drawn wears a moustache or a beard, or is smiling or smoking, because within our groups such traits do not indicate special social roles. For example, within the Hassidic group men with payes or beards are not classified as diversified because these items indicate only membership in the group, not a special social role within the group. If, in some group, a beard were to indicate a special social role or activity, we would classify a drawing having this item in the diversified category, but in none of our groups does a beard indicate a distinctive role.

We speak of classes of men, such as doctors or teachers, rather than drawings of specific men because very few drawings represent specific individuals. Whenever a specific man was drawn, such as the drawing of Morelos, that drawing was put in the diversified category.

Table 7 presents the results of this classification. It will be seen that Heidelberg is by far the highest, with a score of 58 per cent. Edinburgh and the Armenian Lebanese are next, 38 per cent of their drawings representing diversified roles; several other groups score only slightly lower. The Chiapas Indians, the Israeli Orthodox and the Lebanese villages II are lowest with only 1 or 2 per cent of their men depicted in such roles. Any difference of 20 per cent between groups in Table 7 is highly significant ($P < 0.01$) and many smaller differences are significant at the 0.05 level.

Table 8 has been prepared to show that the differences between the three groups highest in diversification and the three lowest groups are consistent. It will be seen that the three highest groups in overall diversity are the highest in several respects. The differences among groups are smallest in respect to religious figures; no group has a high score in this category. The three low groups have zero scores on all counts.

Among the three high groups there are significant differences. In relation to Heidelberg and to the Armenian Lebanese, Edinburgh is low in historical figures (most historical figures consist of Greek, Roman or other ancient warriors). Heidelberg outdoes Edinburgh and the Armenians in modern gunmen, such as cowboys, bandits, and sheriffs. Edinburgh is higher than any other groups in sportsmen, athletes and occupations.

We have noted that Heidelberg exceeds other groups in

Table 7   Per Cents of Drawings Representing Diversified Social Roles

55	Heidelberg	21	Kyoto
*		20	Ankara
*		19	
*		18	Cambodia
38	Edinburgh, Armenian	17	San Cristobal
	Lebanese	16	
37		15	
36	Gothenberg	14	
35	Beirut	13	Japanese village
34	Taipei I	12	Brooklyn Negroes
33		11	
32	Athens	10	Navaho, Mississippi Negroes
31		9	Lebanese villages I
30	Israeli nonorthodox	8	
29		7	Tehran, Brooklyn white Christians
28		6	Brooklyn Yeshivas
27		5	Brooklyn public school Jews, Hassidim
26		4	
25	Taipei II	3	
24		2	Israeli Orthodox, Chiapas Indians
23	Mexico City	1	Lebanese villages II
22			

overall diversification. In previous chapters we have had occasion to mention the versatility of the Heidelberg boys. In the Heidelberg drawings there is a total of twelve ancient warriors, one of whom has been shown earlier (see Figure 54). To counterbalance the military emphasis in our Heidelberg illustrations, Figure 75 presents a professor and Figure 76 an entertainer. More than half of the Heidelberg drawings could be used as illustrations of diversity, but it is not feasible to present so many figures from a single group.

In Table 7, Edinburgh ties with the Armenian Lebanese for second place. Figure 77 shows a Scot at play and Figure 78 a Scot at work; both appear to be having equal fun. Figure 79 is a Scottish fighter. Several of the Armenian Lebanese drawings depict ancient warriors (see Figure 80), and some athletes (Figure 81). Although we have not classified him as a diversified figure, one Armenian apparently loves flowers (Figure 82); he is the only man drawn holding one.

Space does not permit us to illustrate further the forms of diversity except to reproduce drawings of a soccer player from Athens (Figure 83), a patriot from Israel (Figure 84), and a boxer from Cambodia (Figure 85).

The bottom of Tables 7 and 8 show that in many groups the number of drawings depicting distinctive kinds of indi-

Table 8　Percentages of Diversified Social Roles in Six Groups

	Heidel-berg	Edin-burgh	Armenians Lebanese	Israeli Orthodox	Chiapas Indians	Lebanese villages
Historical figures	12	1	17	0	0	0
Modern gunmen	19	5	5	1	0	0
Foreigners	6	3	5	0	0	0
Sportsmen, athletes	12	15	7	0	2	0
Entertainers	4	3	1	0	0	0
Occupations	2	10	1	1	0	0
Religious figures	0	1	2	0	0	0
Total	55	38	38	2	2	0

viduals approaches zero. The American groups rank among the least diversified. In the Brooklyn white Christians drawings only seven figures were classified as having diversified social roles, among the Brooklyn Yeshiva boys only six, and among the Brooklyn public school Jews and the Hassidim only five each. This means, of course, that nearly all Brooklyn boys drew American men in modern clothes, with no other identification. Figures 86 and 87 are reasonably typical.

Why do some groups, such as the Heidelberg, Scottish, and Armenian boys make very diversified drawings, and some groups, including Americans, draw chiefly what are relatively standard figures?

This finding we did not anticipate, and therefore we cannot propose that our theory predicted it, although perhaps it could have done so. From our theory it follows that if some groups of boys are more variable in respect to their values than are boys of other groups their drawings should be more variable in content. There are many persons who would agree with this interpretation, but since it was reached a posteriori we cannot insist that our data give it strong support. We will therefore not attempt a final interpretation of cultural diversity in drawings at the present time but hope that this problem will be further pursued.

Of the low-scoring groups in respect to diversity, it should be noted that several are of the low and lower-middle classes. It is possible that, in general, boys who come from the higher socioeconomic backgrounds make more diversified drawings. This possibility needs to be explored, but it should be kept in mind that the Edinburgh boys and the Armenian Lebanese who have high diversity scores do not have a particularly high socioeconomic status and that the Heidelberg boys' socioeconomic status is not sufficient in itself to account for their high standing. In this respect we remind the reader that American drawings are among the least diverse, although the American standard of living is high. In other words, while standard of living may play a role, it is not sufficient to account for the great range of scores which have been found. It would appear that diversity in social roles depends upon diversity of values, not merely upon prosperity, although the very poor may not envision the possibility of diverse roles to the same extent as the more well-to-do and better educated.

Figure 75   A German professor and his assistant.

Figure 76 *A German entertainer.*

Figure 77   A Scot at play.

Figure 78   A Scot at work.

150

Figure 79   A Scot fighter.

Figure 80   An Armenian warrior.

152

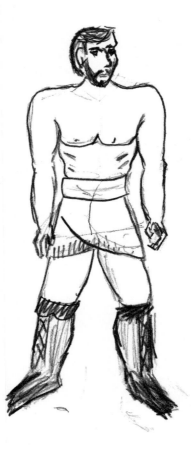

Figure 81   An Armenian athlete.

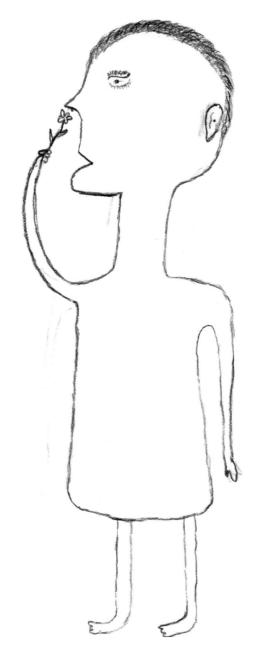

Figure 82   An Armenian with a flower.

154

Figure 83   A Greek athlete.

Figure 84   An Israeli soldier.

Figure 85   A Cambodian boxer.

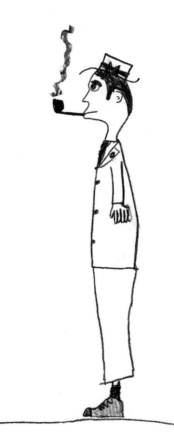

Figure 86   A man drawn by a Brooklyn Yeshiva boy.

158

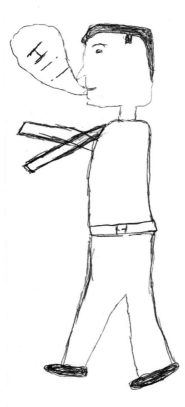

Figure 87   A man drawn by a Brooklyn white Christian boy.

Chapter Eleven

Ridicule and Humor

Up to the present page we have been concerned chiefly with showing that children's drawings usually indicate favorable attitudes toward their referents. We have also indicated that the absence of familiar referents, such as men engaged in work or religious men, probably shows the absence of a strong positive attitude but not necessarily a negative one. That a negative as well as a positive attitude can be expressed in art is not to be denied. It must have occurred to many readers that cartoonists and caricaturists often draw to ridicule. Our experience, however, is that in normal elementary school classrooms ridicule in drawings seldom appears, possibly because ridicule requires more virtuosity in technique and more sophistication of ideas than does the expression of admiration. These qualities may seldom be possessed by grade school pupils. Notwithstanding, a few of the drawings in our collection do seem to have been intended to ridicule, rather than praise. The reader must be aware, however, that he can easily attribute to a child a degree of cleverness or viciousness that he may not really possess.

Since the Heidelberg boys draw so well, one would expect that they would be capable of expressing ridicule, and this expectation is correct. Figure 88 by a German boy probably expresses ridicule of an American sheriff, particularly if one considers the bird and the bird's nest on the sheriff's hat and the sheriff's big feet.

A Swedish drawing of an Englishman (Figure 89) is certainly intended to ridicule; note the smoke coming from the ears, the hook on the fly front of the trousers, the hair below the shorts, and the decorations on the shoes. Another Swedish drawing (Figure 90) is so exaggerated that it undoubtedly expresses disapproval. Figure 91 is the only Scottish attempt at humor, and Figure 92 the only Lebanese Arab example. The Armenian Lebanese drawing, Figure 93, exaggerates the Middle Eastern nose. It is difficult to identify many other drawings as definitely intended to convey ridicule. The Japanese boys, who have excellent art technique, seem to be without humor. This is true also of American, Greek, and Israeli drawings.

To summarize, in our samples of boys' drawings, the frequency of recognizable ridicule and humor is small. Such drawings play only a minor role in children's art except, perhaps, among exceptionally gifted groups. Drawings by children express negative attitudes primarily by omission of subject matter. The predominant mode of expression is positive, and this may be true also for most adults.

Figure 88   An American sheriff drawn by a Heidelberg boy.

162

Figure 89   An Englishman drawn by a Gothenberg boy.

Figure 90   A fat policeman drawn by a Swede.

164

Figure 91   A wind-blown old man drawn by a Scottish boy.

Figure 92   A caricature drawn by a Beirut boy.

Figure 93   A distorted figure drawn by an Armenian Lebanese boy.

167

Chapter Twelve

The Value Hypothesis versus the Familiarity Hypothesis

It is an old saw that children draw what they know. This is a misleading statement because it fails to indicate that there is a considerable degree of selectivity on the part of children in regard to their choices of referents among the many possibilities of subject matter that are available to them.

At various points in the preceding chapters we have taken occasion to note that the men drawn by children, although they must be familiar to the children, represent choices within their realms of familiarity. Some familiar men are drawn and some equally familiar are not drawn.

We are especially aware that accounting for the contents of drawings on the basis of familiarity is very common because in presenting some of the foregoing material orally to individuals and to groups we have frequently encountered this alternative explanation. It must therefore be given serious attention if we propose to maintain that the value hypothesis is superior to it.

In many drawings, the familiarity hypothesis and the value hypothesis are equally tenable, because the data present no conflict between the two interpretations. This was pointed out in Chapter 3 which was concerned with some quasi-universal choices of men. For example, boys of eleven, twelve, and thirteen years draw few men who have only one eye, one ear, one arm, or one leg. Since there are relatively few such men, their scarcity in drawings *may* be due to their infrequency. On the other hand, that they are not drawn may also be due to the fact that crippled and maimed men are not goal figures.

However, there are many situations in which the two interpretative principles lead not to the same but to different predictions concerning the contents of children's drawings. We propose here to summarize the data already presented concerning the contents of drawings for which the two hypotheses lead us to expect different results. We believe the evidence will be found unequivocally in favor of the value hypothesis.

Before we begin this review of the evidence we should note that the familiarity hypothesis takes two different forms. It sometimes refers to the child's familiarity with real men (in the flesh); it may also refer to his familiarity with representations of men whom he has never seen in the flesh, such as Indians, figures in comic books, and historical figures. Both forms of this hypothesis must be examined.

Let us begin by reviewing some of the material in Chapter 4 which has to do with the relative frequencies of depictions of men in modern dress and in traditional dress. In all cities boys primarily draw men in modern dress. This fact cannot serve as proof of either alternative interpretation, since in most cities modern dress is familiar and is also socially approved.

There are several instances, however, in which certain ethnic forms of dress are very familiar and yet are seldom drawn. For example, among Navaho Indians in 1936 the native male costume was much more often worn than modern dress; nevertheless, Navaho boys in Navaho schools drew modern dress in 75 per cent of the cases. Jewish boys in Yeshiva parochial schools in Brooklyn wear skullcaps in school. They presumably do so at home, and it is likely that their fathers and other male relatives also wear them, but only 3 per cent of the Yeshiva boys drew a man with a skull-cap. Among the Hassidim in Brooklyn, only 35 per cent of the drawings of classifiable costume portrayed a costume that was primarily traditional (Figure 94). Hassidic drawings of modern men may be explained by their familiarity with modern dress, the familiarity-in-art hypothesis cannot explain the presence of Hassidic figures, because the Hassidic tradition excludes representation of the human figure, that is, there is no traditional way of drawing Hassidic men or other men. Negroes outnumber Hassidim in the Bedford-Stuyvesant area of Brooklyn where our Hassidic boys live, but no Hassidic boy drew a Negro. It is, of course, not possible to show an illustration of this point.

Reviewing further the evidence that certain kinds of familiar men are not drawn, we note that among Ladino boys in San Cristobal, Mexico, no Indian costumes were drawn, although a check experiment showed that Ladinos can draw Indians in native costume. They are familiar; because Indians are constantly present in the streets of San Cristobal. They outnumber Ladinos in the State of Chiapas, in which San Cristobal is located. Furthermore, school textbooks, which are prescribed nationally by the federal government, contain representations of Indians as well as of Ladinos.

The situation of the Zinecanteco and Chamula Indian schoolboys, near San Cristobal, is even more striking than that of the Ladino boys. The Indian boys and the men of their villages wear Indian costumes. Yet 70 per cent of these boys draw men in modern dress; only 30 per cent draw men in native dress. Cultural conflict in respect to values can account for this division, but the principle of familiarity cannot. It should be noted that in the villages of these boys there are no placard advertisements, no comic books, no newspapers, no magazines, no movies which could provide representations of Western men as art models, and no Ladinos live in most of the villages, yet they are the predominant referents of drawings.

To continue; in the large cities of Sudan (Khartoum and Omdurman) in which predominantly galabias are seen on the street only 15 per cent of the drawings represent men in galabias. In a Japanese village in which most of the men wear native costumes only 9 per cent of the drawings represent men in local dress. The familiarity hypothesis cannot account for such results.

Chapter 5 dealt with the representation of physical features, some of which are racial, and some of which, such as hair styles and moustaches, are in part cultural. It was found that Caucasians and Asiatics draw, respectively, Caucasians and Asiatics in almost all cases. However, American Negroes, even those living in segregated areas and attending all-Negro schools, very seldom draw Negroes; the persons drawn are Caucasians. Of course, Negro boys in Negro neighborhoods and Negro schools see Negro men more often than they see white men. What about the relative frequencies of representations of Negroes and whites in mass media such as newspapers, magazines, movies, and television programs? In New York, at least, there are many window displays, magazine illustrations, and placards aimed particularly at Negroes, but they usually portray Negroes whose Negroid physical traits are minimized. In this instance the frequency of representations has some plausibility as an explanation for the drawing of white men by Negro boys, but the data are not decisive. We have found no integrated classroom or integrated community in which Negroes predominate where either white or Negro children draw Negroes.

Chapter 6 was concerned with indices of masculinity. Although the Heidelberg and Mexico City boys drew a greater number of masculine figures than do American boys, it is doubtful that Germans and Mexicans have wider shoulders, bigger muscles, or carry more knives and guns than do Americans. Masculinity is probably in the mind rather than in the flesh. It is interesting that German boys drew more American Indians than did Mexican Ladinos and boys in the

United States. What can the familiarity hypothesis do with this? That American boys who see many Western movies seldom draw Indians is presumably due to the fact that in movies Indians are usually the "bad men" and usually are depicted half-naked, painted, and of low social status. In other words the infrequency of Indians in American drawings confirms the value hypothesis.

The portrayal of occupations was discussed in Chapter 8. It was noted that few men are drawn who are engaged in any kind of work or who wear occupational insignia. This applies to men whose appearance and vocational indentification are necessarily familiar to boys, including the drivers of the buses in which boys ride, the policemen directing traffic at street crossings near schools, and barbers, dentists, and doctors, all of whom most boys must necessarily patronize. In respect to mass media it should be noted that policemen, dentists, and doctors are frequently portrayed in advertisements, in movies, on television, and in picture books. Therefore, not only the men themselves but also representations of them are familiar to most children in modern cities. Thus, the familiarity hypothesis cannot account for the comparative absence of such men in drawings. Their unpopularity with teen-age boys, not their unfamiliarity, must be responsible for their low per cent of occurrence in drawings.

In short, in all instances in which the familiarity hypothesis and the value hypothesis are in conflict, the latter wins. Although boys draw only men of whom they have some knowledge, either real or pictorial (that is, they seldom create imaginary men), among the many kinds of men with whom they are acquainted in life or in art, they most often draw men who represent the positive values of themselves and their respective societies.

Figure 94   An Hassidic man drawn by an Hassidic boy.

Chapter Thirteen

A Review of
Group Differences

The preceding chapters have been organized by content, that is, each chapter has discussed the frequencies in various groups of items such as modern dress, traditional dress, racial features, and smiling. Such an organization of data necessarily scatters among various chapters the information concerning any group. We propose now to reassemble the data in order to characterize the drawings of each group or of related sets of groups.

In doing this we will arrange the groups geographically, as we have done previously. Whereas we appear to be listing nations, the titles of our groups do not imply that we can characterize any nation as a whole. We are not proposing that our findings in any country are representative of that country for we did not obtain samples of drawings with that in mind. Our aim in collecting drawings was to achieve a heterogeneity of groups within the limits of our time and resources. Although it was not possible, in this study, to collect drawings that could be assumed to be representative of the countries from which they came, it may be that in some cases they will prove representative.

The data to be considered in this chapter, for the most part, have already been presented in Tables 1 to 8. Occasionally additional data not contained in these tables will be discussed.

174

The American Groups

From the United States, we have seven main groups which contributed 665 drawings. Five groups are from the New York area. This overloading of New York is due in part to its being our place of residence, but also in part to the factors being studied; we were seeking heterogeneity and New York is made up of heterogeneous racial and religious groups. Besides New York, the American groups include Mississippi Negroes and Navaho Indians. In addition to the main American groups we have smaller sets of data from Long Island, Maryland, Washington, D.C., Pennsylvania, and Kansas. These sets of drawings are not labeled as "main groups" because they are made up of fewer than one hundred drawings, and because some of the children in these groups are below age eleven.

The American Majority Group

We will begin with a consideration of the drawings of what may be called the American majority group, that is, white Christians of European origin. This is not the majority group in several New York City boroughs or in some other parts of the United States, but it is the majority group for the United States as a whole.

The pictures drawn by various white Christian groups of Americans are relatively uniform. For one thing, they are uniform in that they represent Caucasians. Seldom does an American white Christian draw a Negro, an Eskimo, a Chinese, a Japanese, or an American Indian. This agrees with the finding that Americans are low in the production of drawings of what we have called diversified social roles. A boy of the American majority group seldom draws men belonging to an era, a country, a religion, an ethnic group, or a race other than his own. The typical American boy does not draw men of historical importance, whether from his own country, or of foreign lands. Representations of American Indians are familiar to him because their pictures are present in geography and history books and in movies, yet he seldom draws them. There is much else that can be said about what the majority group American boy does *not* draw or seldom draws. He seldom or never draws religious figures, masculine figures, military men, men at work or in occupational settings.

What, then, does he draw? Chiefly, he draws well-dressed, modern, young men who stand before the viewer, smiling, but doing nothing. This is a rather vacuous picture of present-day American youth, but we are obligated to describe what we have found. As we have noted, our samples may not be representative, but, insofar as positive values are discernible in the drawings of the American majority group, they seem to represent two things: first, self-esteem, that is, Americans draw themselves; and second, hedonism, that is, they draw many smiling figures. There is little or no evidence of a concern with work, with religion, with individual achievement, with participation in sports, or with unusual social roles. Figure 95 may be said to be typical of the drawings of boys of the American majority group in respect to its paucity of content.

New York Jewish Groups

We have drawings from three New York Jewish groups: Jewish boys in public schools, Yeshiva boys, and Hassidic boys. We doubt that more than a few drawings of the first two groups could be distinguished from drawings of the Brooklyn white Christians. For example, can the reader decide which group drew Figure 96? (Answer: Group 5) Like New York representatives of the majority American group, New York Jewish boys draw few working men, few athletes, few sportsmen, few foreigners, few men with distinctive social roles, few men with pipes, cigars, canes, beards, and moustaches. From drawings, it would appear that only three Jewish men in two hundred wear skullcaps. In other words, American Jewish drawings seem to be thoroughly Americanized. The one distinction seems to be that Jewish boys draw fewer men who are smiling than do white Christian boys.

The Hassidim differ from the other Jewish groups only in that they draw more men with skullcaps and draw some Hassidic hats, payes, and beards. In other respects, we find no differences between the nonorthodox and ultraconservative boys. In the majority of Hassidic drawings, men are not in Hassidic costume. In the Hassidic drawings, as in other drawings, there is no representation of prayer or of religious observances.

American Negro Groups

We have presented data from a group of Negroes in Brooklyn and from a group in Mississippi. In addition we have drawings from Negro children in Maryland and from students in a Negro university. As in the Jewish groups, the Negro drawings differ little from drawings made by the American majority group. The Mississippi drawings are somewhat "poorer" in terms of drawing skill, and fewer of the men in Mississippi Negro drawings are smiling. There is among them the same paucity of workers, of clergymen, of athletes, of masculine emphasis, and of men whose social, vocational, or avocational roles are discernible.

Nearly all the Negro drawings clearly represent white men, as do other American drawings; few represent Negroes. This finding strongly supports the theory that drawings represent goal figures and that in appearance, and perhaps in other things, the American Negro wishes to be a Caucasian. Insofar as the evidence from drawings is concerned, American Negro goals are not different from those of whites. A relatively typical Mississippi drawing is presented in Figure 97.

Navaho Indians

The Navaho Indian drawings were obtained by the late Dr. Morris Steggerda in 1936. It is interesting to note that in 1936, when nearly all Navaho men were wearing Navaho dress, the majority of the Navaho boys drew men in modern dress (see Figure 98 for an illustration). In conformity with the American pattern, very few of these drawings show a man in a specialized role, such as a teacher, a policeman, or a farmer, except for a considerable number depicting men in Navaho costume.

In brief, in the United States there is much in common between the drawings of white Christians, Jews, Negroes, and Navahos. The idea that American culture manages to achieve a uniform set of values is strongly supported by our data.

Mexican Drawings

From Mexico we have three main groups. One group combines lower and higher socioeconomic groups in Mexico City. Although they have some Indian ancestry, they show no evidence of retention of Indian culture, for their culture is European rather than Indian. In most parts of Mexico such people are called Ladinos. The second group consists of Ladino boys in San Cristobal, Chiapas, 800 miles south of Mexico City. All members of this group, like those in Mexico City, should be classified as Americo-European in culture.

In the Mexico City drawings and in the San Cristobal drawings all of the men drawn are Caucasian. Figure 99 is a fairly typical drawing from Mexico City, and Figure 100 from San Cristobal. As illustrations, they could be interchanged. In other respects, too, the San Cristobal drawings appear to differ but little from those in Mexico City. The frequency of smiling faces is 12 per cent in the former in comparison with 15 per cent in the latter, an insignificant difference. The number of San Cristobal drawings scored as showing masculine emphasis is 37 per cent, compared to 50 per cent in Mexico City. The frequency of distinguishable social roles in San Cristobal is 17 per cent, in Mexico City 23 per cent. These scores for masculinity and diversification of social roles for both Mexican cities are above those of the United States groups.

We will see later that the drawings from Mexico City and San Cristobal resemble those of several European cities more closely then they resemble those of the United States. It seems likely that they resemble Spain most closely, but we have no drawings from Spain with which to determine this point.

The third Mexican group consists of Indian boys, wearing Indian costumes, speaking Indian languages, and living in primitive agricultural communities near San Cristobal in the State of Chiapas. They are, however, attending schools, unlike many other Indian boys in Chiapas.

The drawings of these Zinecanteco and Chamula Indian boys who live near San Cristobal provide a sharp contrast to those of the Ladino Mexican groups just discussed. In emphasis upon masculinity the Ladino groups are high, but among the Indian boys it is low (3 per cent). Among the Indians the portrayal of distinctive social roles is lower than among the Ladinos. Smiling, too, in Indian drawings has a low frequency (5 per cent). In fact, in most of our tables the drawings of the Zinecanteco and Chamula Indian boys are among the two or three lowest groups. This is partly because their drawings are so "primitive." A figure which shows the poverty of content in a Zinecanteco drawing is shown in Figure 101.

Do these groups score low on value scales because their drawings are so poor? Their low artistic proficiency may play a role, but drawings from other groups show that not much proficiency is required to draw a smile, a moustache, a pistol, or a knife. One or more of these is relevant to the score on several scales, but they were seldom drawn by these Indian boys. All Zinecantecos and Chamulas wear hats, but only 22 per cent draw hats. Only 9 per cent drew the native tunic which is worn by all and which can be recognized even in a poor drawing (see Figure 102). Furthermore, when asked to draw a Chamula or a Zinecanteco, nearly all can do so.

The Zinecanteco and Chamula drawings are so low in content that one is tempted to guess that the boys of this group are very unsure of their social goals. Since Indians are not accepted by the Ladinos, the Indian boys are probably dubious of the values of their own groups and unsure that they will be permitted to accept Ladinos' values. In any case, it is clear that the transmission of social values from Ladinos to Indians in Chiapas after four hundred years of living side by side has been slight.

European Drawings

The European drawings are from Scotland, Gothenberg (Sweden), Heidelberg, and Athens. In discussing Europeans, we shall include the nonorthodox boys of Tel Aviv and Haifa since they are of recent European derivation. The Ladinos of Mexico might well be included, but they have already been discussed.

In several respects there is considerable similarity among the European groups. For example, they draw white men in almost all cases, and most of the men drawn are in modern dress. In masculine emphasis they vary from high (71 per cent in Heidelberg) to intermediate (26 per cent in Israel), but none of the European groups is very low in masculinity. In respect to the frequency of smiling in drawings, European groups are below the urban American groups, but all except Athens are higher than the Middle Eastern groups.

In the number of drawings which represent a man playing a specialized social role all European groups are high (Heidelberg, 59 per cent; Edinburgh, 38 per cent; Gothenberg, 38 per cent; Athens, 32 per cent; Tel Aviv and Haifa, 30 per cent). In contrast, the highest American score in this category is 12 per cent.

We suggest that Figure 103 from Gothenberg represents a typical European drawing because the man drawn is white, wears a modern costume, and is engaged in a masculine activity. If he is smiling, it is only slightly. We are unable to account for the missing forearm, except as an artist's oversight.

In brief, what generally distinguishes the European groups from Americans are their high masculinity and high diversity scores, and moderate smiling scores. Since there is considerable agreement in these respects between cities as far apart as Mexico City and Tel Aviv, it seems likely that these aspects of European culture are widespread. It should be noted, however, that we have not sampled rural or village groups in Europe.

The Middle East

The Middle East earns its name because it lies between Europe and Asia. In this area our groups consist of one from Ankara, one from Beirut, two from Arab villages in Lebanon, an Armenian group in Lebanon, a group of Orthodox village boys in Israel, and one group in Tehran, Iran.

In some respects, drawings of these groups do not differ much from the drawings of European groups and could be grouped with them. All consist of Caucasians, and nearly all draw Caucasians. In the main, they draw men in Western dress. The frequencies of smiling in drawings is lower, however, than it is in most European groups and much lower than in most American groups. Only the Mississippi Negroes, the Athenians, and the Chiapas Indians rate equally low. Masculine emphasis in drawings is relatively low but not extremely low in Middle Eastern groups (Lebanese villages I,

24; Ankara, 22; Israeli Orthodox, 20; Tehran, 17; Lebanese villages II, 15 per cent). In this respect, only Beirutis and the Armenian Lebanese are equal to European groups. In general, as we have noted earlier, the Beirutis and the Armenians score much as do Europeans.

In diversity of social roles, Ankara, Beirut, Tehran, and Lebanese Arab villages score much as do most United States groups. This similarity between these Middle Eastern and the American groups may be the result of more than one cause. American groups are acquainted with varied occupational, professional, and recreational roles, but apparently prefer uniformity. In some parts of the Middle East, particularly among the rural groups, the knowledge of variation in social roles may be quite limited.

All in all, it would seem that the Middle Eastern groups are oriented toward European goals but have not fully accepted them. This interpretation would explain their relatively low position in respect to hedonism, masculinity, and individuality.

Eastern Asia

There remain for consideration the data from Cambodia, Japan, and Taiwan. In all these countries boys draw men mostly with Asiatic features, even though they have been widely exposed to Western people and to Western movies. The Taiwanese alone draw Caucasian features to any considerable degree, but only 15 per cent of all classifiable Taiwanese drawings represent white men. All three national groups chiefly draw men who wear modern rather than traditional costumes, but of the three the Taiwanese drew the largest number of traditional costumes.

There are interesting differences between these three nations in regard to the number of modern military men depicted. We have devoted no chapter to modern military men, because in most groups the number of modern military figures is small. In Cambodia, in 100 drawings, the incidence is zero. Among the 200 Japanese drawings, the number is zero; among the 200 Taiwanese it is 27 per cent (see Figure 104). The difference between the Cambodians and the Japanese on the one hand and the Taiwanese on the other is statistically significant. It probably reflects significant social differences. In no other group but the Taiwanese does the number of modern military men exceed 4 per cent. We are informed by Professor Ivan London of Brooklyn College, who is a student of Chinese culture and who recently visited Taiwan, that since Taiwan lives as an armed camp the Taiwanese government has engaged in a massive campaign to magnify the honor and dignity of soldiers in the eyes of the younger generation.

Besides the differences in the frequency of men in modern military uniforms shown in drawings by the Far Eastern groups, there are other distinctions between the drawings of these groups. No Cambodian and only one Japanese figure carried a weapon. Among the Taiwanese drawings, in addition to 27 per cent of modern military men, another 8 per cent have non-military weapons, usually a knife (see Figure 105 for an example). In all, 35 per cent of the men drawn by the Taiwanese are modern military men or carry modern weapons; no other group has a comparable record.

In frequencies of smiling the East Asian group drawings lie between 31 and 21 per cent, that is, they are in the intermediate range, with the American urban groups generally higher and the Middle Eastern groups generally lower. In scores on diversification of social roles, groups in these three nations hold intermediate positions relative to European and Middle Eastern groups.

To summarize, there appear to be differences revealed by drawings which, broadly speaking, distinguish culture areas. But within a culture area it also appears that there are regional, perhaps local differences.

Figure 95   A drawing by a Brooklyn white christian boy.

Figure 96 A drawing by another American.

185

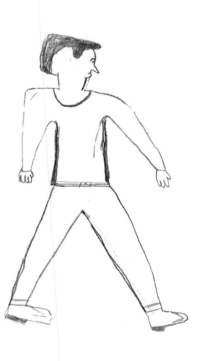

Figure 97   A drawing by a Mississippi Negro.

186

Figure 98   A drawing by a Navaho Indian.

Figure 99   A drawing by a Mexico City boy.

188

Figure 100   A drawing by a San Cristobal boy.

Figure 101   A drawing by a Zinecanteco Indian boy.

190

Figure 102   A drawing by another Zinecanteco Indian boy.

Figure 103   A drawing by a Gothenberg boy.

192

Figure 104   A Taiwanese military drawing.

Figure 105   A Taiwanese drawing of a Western man.

194

Chapter Fourteen

Women Drawn by Girls

We come now to the penultimate chapter. The reader has had an opportunity to look at 105 drawings of men made by boys. We ask him now to look at some women drawn by girls. Our data on this topic are not extensive, but we believe that girls' drawings lead to the same conclusion as do boys' drawings, that drawings represent group values.

The girls who drew came from the Sudan, Mississippi, Japan, Iran, the Hopi reservation, Turkey, and Israel. This is a very miscellaneous collection. In general, girls' drawings of women were obtained when there was an interlude in our more systematic collection of drawings of men or when, despite our instructions, girls drew women, and we decided to accept their work. We present these somewhat haphazard data, partly to amuse, but chiefly to suggest that the principles which govern the drawings of boys also govern the drawings of girls.

For example, just as no American white boy drew a Negro man, so no American white girl drew a Negro woman, although a Negro Sudanese girl did (see Figure 106). Among the Mississippi Negroes neither boys nor girls drew a Negro. Figure 107, drawn by a Mississippi Negro girl, appears to be, for girls, the feminine counterpart of masculine emphasis.

The drawings of Japanese girls are demure (see Figure 108).

No Tehran boy drew a peasant in traditional costume. In Tehran a modification of the traditional feminine costume, the *chadura,* is still worn by many women over modern dress. In more than two hundred drawings of women made by

195

Iranian girls the only drawing of a chadura is that shown in
Figure 109. The contrast between the old and the new is
sharp in Tehran. Figure 110 represents a woman who was
described by the girl who drew her as "a lady I saw in the
street." It did not seem wise to inquire as to what she meant.

Let us show the drawings made by two Hopi Indian girls
from the same village (Figures 111 and 112). It is clear that
Hopi girls, like Hopi boys, have their allegiances divided between traditional and modern dress.

Girls of Ankara, Turkey, admire good looks, just as other
girls do; Figures 113 and 114 represent two women drawn by
Turkish girls. A black and white reproduction does not show
it, but the woman in Figure 113 has golden hair. Foreign aid
has not yet produced such blondes in Ankara.

Figure 115 was drawn by an Orthodox Israeli girl. It
shows that the eyes are as important as the body as feminine
enticements.

Figure 116, drawn by a nonorthodox Israeli girl, is our
last illustration of values in drawings. It shows that perhaps,
after all, we have paid too much attention to groups and too
little to individuality.

Figure 106   A Sudanese drawing of a woman.

Figure 107   A woman drawn by a Mississippi Negro girl.

198

Figure 108   A woman drawn by a Japanese girl.

Figure 109   *The only woman in a chadura drawn by a Tehran girl.*

Figure 110   A modern woman drawn by a Tehran girl.

Figure 111   A Hopi woman drawn by a Hopi girl.

Figure 112   A modern woman drawn by a Hopi girl.

Figure 113   A blond Turkish woman.

204

Figure 114   A shapely Turkish woman.

Figure 115   An expressive face (Tel Aviv).

206

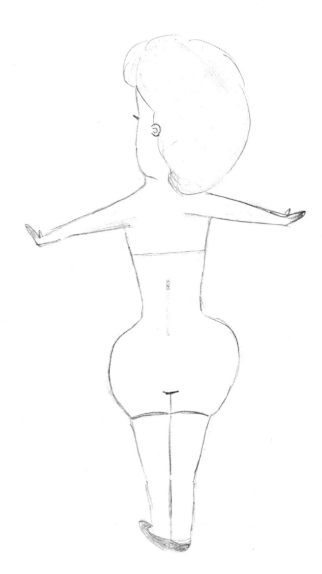

Figure 116   A backward view (Haifa).

207

Chapter Fifteen

Some Future Prospects

In the first chapter we proposed the theory that children's drawings represent social values. In later chapters we presented in support of this theory evidence from a heterogenous assortment of groups. We have also compared the evidence for the value hypothesis with that for the familiarity hypothesis, which seems at present to be the only competitor. It should be clear that what we have done is only a beginning. What remains is to sketch out very briefly what should be done and what can be done in the future.

What is needed most is more "validation." This word usually means that a proposed measure or index, such as the frequencies of the contents of drawings, should be checked against well-established measures of the same referent, which in this case concerns social values. The main obstacle is that there are for children no established, accepted techniques which yield categories of values comparable to ours.

Perhaps a solution can be found by eventually developing a means of translating one scheme of values to another, but this is indeed a formidable future task. It would mean an achievement on the part of the behavioral sciences of something comparable to Newton's universal law of gravitation. While awaiting such a solution, we suggest that the student of values proceed to emulate the early explorers and naturalists who did not attempt to achieve celestial truth but wished chiefly to advance our knowledge of the earth and its inhabitants.

We believe that collecting drawings has something in common with collecting plants for an herbarium. The dried and pressed plants are not alive, but they serve usefully in studying the plants which exist in the living world. Drawings can perform a similar service for human psychology. We believe they will prove to be useful, even though they do not provide omniscience.

As we have said earlier, few methods of approaching behavior are so widely applicable. In our experience, drawings of a man and drawings of many other referents can be obtained almost everywhere. It is no new finding that there is an almost universal interest in graphic representation. Often there are taboos with respect to what shall be represented; in that case, the tabooed as well as the nontabooed subjects can be simultaneously investigated. Future studies of drawings, much wider than ours, can provide growing points for field studies in behavioral science, which needs not one but many such growing points.

Studies of the Negro areas of Africa may provide an example. With so many tribal groups, so many languages, so many conflicting influences, it is difficult to obtain an understanding of the many values, attitudes, and loyalties which exist there. Certainly, the printed psychological tests devised for college students in America are not suited to the jungle or the bush. Something as simple as human figure drawings may provide leads which cannot be obtained from more sophisticated techniques. Let us recall that the first geographical surveys of Africa were not made by U-2 flights. Primitive situations often require the use of simple implements in the early phases of exploration. The utility of the drawing technique lies in its simplicity and its ability to suggest interpretations, which we believe we have demonstrated.

Our suggestion that it can be used in relatively underdeveloped areas, such as sub-Saharan Africa, should not obscure the fact that it can also be used in the most highly developed countries. We believe the previous chapters have shown this. The drawing method is *par excellence* a comparative method of very wide applicability, applicable to both primitive and advanced social groups.

For this reason we suggest that drawings be used to measure some of the social changes in attitudes and values which occur in the course of modernization, acculturation, and educational and economic advancement. By the systematic collection of drawings at decade or semidecade intervals, valuable data on social change could be obtained. In a few instances, as with the Navaho Indians from whom drawings were obtained thirty years ago, a base for a long-term, follow-up investigation of changes in the content of drawings is already available.

We have proposed only a few of the ideas which have occurred to us in respect to the possible uses to which the analysis of the contents of children's art can be put. They are intended only to be suggestive. If the direction of our work is pursued by others, imaginatively and soundly, nothing will please us more.

Bibliography

Badri, M. B., and Dennis, W., "Human Figure Drawings in Relation to Modernization in the Sudan," *J. of Psychol.*, **58** (1964), 421–425.

Dennis, W., "The Human Figure Drawings of Bedouins," *J. Soc. Psychol.*, **52** (1960), 209–219.

Goodenough, F. L., *The Measurement of Intelligence by Drawings*, Yonkers-on-Hudson, World Book Co., 1926.

Keizo, S., *Japanese Life and Culture in the Meiji Era*, Tokyo, Obunsha, 1958.

Machover, K., *Personality Projection in the Drawing of the Human Figure*, Springfield, Ill., C. C. Thomas, 1949.

Myrdal, G., *An American Dilemma*, New York, Harper and Bros., 1944.

Poll, S., *The Hasidic Community of Williamsburg*, New York, Free Press of Glencoe, 1962.